What are people s

Be Visionary

As a commercial banker focused on the U.S. Middle-Market, I witness daily the struggle for visionary strategic leadership. I worked under Marty's leadership for five years in a fast-growth company during a time of upheaval—particularly surrounding the way our customers selected their vendors. Marty transformed the company through the creation and implementation of a pivot strategy that led to rapid growth, sustainability, and lucrative and valuable relationships with our customers. This while our competitors faltered. I vividly remember each room in the company's main offices having large dry-erase boards covered with brainstorming insights. I also remember Marty's presence, frequently checking our progress. He was capable of quickly crystallizing the essence of the problem at hand, applying vision, and leading us to develop a winning strategy. He accomplished this on the micro level among our teams and the macro level as the President of the company. *Be Visionary* is a must read for developing and experienced managers and leaders in business. Marty brings a rare intersection of experience in life with special operations, finance, and C-Suite business leadership. Combine these with his creativity and energy, and it's obvious why he's the master—if the student is ready to learn.
Marcus Boggs, Senior Vice President Well Fargo Commercial Bank, LtCol, USMC (retired)

Of the many business books attempting to transpose applicable military leadership skills onto the corporate world, *Be Visionary*—Marty Strong's second successful-business leadership book—should hold pride of place on your bookshelf. In clear and precise terms, he lays out an easy-to-follow methodology for

C-Suite executives, aspirational senior executives, or ambitious mid-level managers planning their rise to the top. His message is as simple as it is impactful: leaders need to take risks to resolve their bias for inaction. They must also be willing to commit themselves to winning for weeks, months, even years, before success is achieved. While there is no guarantee of success, Marty Strong has provided a readable and relatable series of lessons learned and vignettes that encourages the reader to think and act beyond his or her in-box. I've worked with Marty in multiple business sectors, and I know his methodical and instructive leadership process works. Leading teams to the attainment of a great vision isn't for the faint of heart, but for those up to the challenge, read *Be Visionary*. I assure you it will become a weathered and much highlighted learning reference for years to come.

Charles Thomas Rushworth III
Colonel, United States Marine Corp, Retired
Former Professor, U.S. Naval War College – Strategic Studies
Former Healthcare Industry Corporate President

Be Visionary

Strategic Leadership in the Age of Optimization

Be Visionary

Strategic Leadership in the Age of Optimization

Marty Strong

£$
BUSINESS
BOOKS

Winchester, UK
Washington, USA

JOHN HUNT PUBLISHING

First published by Business Books, 2022
Business Books is an imprint of John Hunt Publishing Ltd., No. 3 East St., Alresford, Hampshire SO24 9EE, UK
office@jhpbooks.com
www.johnhuntpublishing.com
www.johnhuntpublishing.com/business-books

For distributor details and how to order please visit the 'Ordering' section on our website.

ISBN: 978 1 78535 432 8
978 1 78535 433 5 (ebook)
Library of Congress Control Number: 2021949278

A CIP catalogue record for this book is available from the British Library.

Design: Matthew Greenfield

UK: Printed and bound by CPI Group (UK) Ltd, Croydon, CR0 4YY
Printed in North America by CPI GPS partners

Contents

Other Books by Marty Strong

Be Nimble – How the Navy SEAL Creative Mindset Wins on the Battlefield and in Business

John Hunt Publishing ISBN-13: 978-1789048407

Preface

We didn't see it coming. The global COVID-19 pandemic took everyone by surprise, a true black swan event of epic proportions. Successfully reacting to crisis is laudable, but proactively anticipating and preparing for crisis—before the damage is done—is a primary function of effective leadership. Strategic thinking across all human enterprise has declined in the last twenty years. Technology now allows us to see the micro and incremental execution outcomes in near real time, and it is mesmerizing. Why risk thinking big thoughts about the future when you can be a champion of optimization today?

Optimization, enabled by the ever-improving science of measurement, has defined strategy as optimization. This trend shortens horizons and creates a management atmosphere, focused on immediate and incremental gratification. A side effect of this focal length is a lack of robust investment. To invest, you must see the future, contemplate the possibilities, and conceive a plan to avoid the threat or seize the opportunity shimmering on the far horizon.

This book's message is focused toward current or aspiring leaders operating in any type of organization. The powerful value of visionary leadership transcends industries, markets, and cultures. It's not too late to bring back deep thinking. Creative thought processes can be reignited; they must be reignited so we can all anticipate and solve the exciting challenges waiting just around the next corner. This narrative is about taking the time to clear and open your mind to the world around you and the world to come. Enjoy this vision quest!

Forward

Shattered and dejected, almost spent, Marty summoned the strength to pull himself up from the muck realizing he had more to give. He marshaled energy from the deep recesses of his mind and body and pushed forward to success, finally becoming a Navy SEAL. Pressing on, Marty achieved personal and professional victories, swiftly moving forward to creatively dominate his testosterone-fueled, monolithic special operations universe. Then, after years of making hay of America's enemies, he smoothly transitioned into the business world with great passion and fortitude.

Marty Strong embodies the American Hero stereotype. From essentially raising himself as a young teen, to becoming a Navy SEAL, to standing at the top of the corporate mountain as the Chief Executive Officer of several companies. Marty is practically impossible to kill, he analyzes everything, challenges his employees to be better, and has good hair. His insights into business success are leveraged daily throughout many organizations. These insights provide a sound foundation for the continuous change required to respond to both consumers and business customers in today's frantic and demanding markets. In this book, you will be honored to peruse the methodical mind of a commercial genius. Marty eloquently composes and intertwines operational stories with tried-and-true business concepts that have been etched in stone with bloodied fingers over the many years of his multi-faceted leadership career.

Be Visionary: Strategic Leadership in the Age of Optimization, is an exceptionally written tome designed to open the eyes of the reader to the reality of business today. You will be introduced to the Vision concept and given an opportunity to build a foundation for leadership success before diving into trends, threats, and opportunities—all while learning how to set a course and communicate your own dynamic vision. His narrative is inculcated with discussions on relevant ethics. These discussions spotlight the increasing challenges experienced by senior managers, as more and more companies, and individuals, skirt customary moral leadership acts and neglect a fundamental duty to protect people—even while actively working to capture short-term profits or market share. The fact that Marty has the guts to talk about "Doing What's Right", in a rudderless, media-driven cultural environment, is inspiring. Another key concept rarely tackled, and beautifully laid-out in his book, is the rampant anxiety paralyzing businesses today. Marty dovetails his experience running complex and highly dangerous military operations with how to adjust your strategic vison and insights to cope with our everchanging business markets. He explains how to lead in competitive arenas where the rules constantly change, and he effectively drives home the point that fear induced decision paralysis can be greatly reduced, even eliminated, through self-awareness and purposeful, repetitive risk taking. This attitude—coupled with his focus on regular, thoughtful planning around potential long-term threats and opportunities—opens a universe of possibilities for leaders today. Marty's enthusiastic voice poses a challenge to risk-averse leadership. Steering away from advice to 'close the castle doors', his guidance transforms hesitant management into an opportunity-harvesting operation, directed by creative and forward-thinking leaders.

Throughout the book, the smart grouping of categories will help generate more visionary thought from tomorrow's business executives. As an CEO, I look at budding Vice Presidents today and realize it should be mandatory for them to read Marty's concepts—to aid in a more enlightened business development approach, and to groom their ability to successfully take over and run large, ever-scaling business organizations. All leaders should have access to the immense amount of business knowledge in *Be Visionary: Strategic Leadership in the Age of Optimization*. Marty Strong's successful career, insightful leadership, and uncanny ability to see the essence of things, are delivered in an exemplary writing style. Warm, direct, honest. I consider this book a key reference unparalleled in its usefulness, for organizations today, and well into the future.

Lee Priest

Chief Executive Officer – ETAK Systems

Georgia Tech Engineer

Harvard Business School Graduate

Author of over 50 patents and the books *Drone Flights* and *Hot Spots*

Acknowledgments

Writing is a humbling experience. The dark side of being a writer is to suffer in solitude, wondering, even as you toil, if anything pouring out of your brain will be perceived as valuable. I've been lucky by having so many close, personal advocates and supporters. People who listen to my musings and lagging self-confidence and then guide me back to why I began writing in the first place. To help others learn through my experiences, good and bad, so they might exceed they're dreams and aspirations. As always, I couldn't have finished this project without the loving support and commitment of my wife Michele. She understands me like no one else. I'd also like to say thanks to Chuck Rushworth and Lee Priest, two intelligent and amazing leaders and successful business executives, who help me keep my message crisp and clear throughout *Be Visionary*. Winning is often all about the quality of your team, and I have a great one!

Chapter One

The Vision Thing

All men dream: but not equally. Those who dream by night in the dusty recesses of their minds wake in the day to find that it was vanity: but the dreamers of the day are dangerous men, for they may act out their dream with open eyes, to make it possible.
T.E. Lawrence

I believe most people who know me, work with me, or have worked with me, would say I have the vision thing—a knack for seeing the future conceptually and placing the present and the past in context with that future. I don't know if it is an acquired capability or a natural talent; but it has been a part of my thinking process, and therefore my leadership style, for an awfully long time.

If I performed an honest self-assessment at this point in my life, I'd say the most valuable thing I add to the equation is an ability to identify and contemplate alternative paths forward. I have plenty of smart and capable technical experts, managers, and creative people working for and with me every day. But the vision thing. That's my ace in the hole, the reason I continue to influence successful business outcomes.

In my book, *Be Nimble – How the Navy SEAL Mindset Wins on the Battlefield and in Business*, I strived to address a wide range of challenges faced by today's business leaders. It felt like the right message: a nimble leader can become wildly successful by applying the techniques and unique leadership mindset used by the elite special operations community and by the Navy SEALs.

I spent twenty happy years in "the teams," as the organization is lovingly called by its alumni—first as an enlisted man and then as an officer. In my first ten years, following both good and bad leaders, I learned just as much about planning, leading, and executing as I did while leading these elite warriors for the following decade. Like most of society, the natural abilities and talents were dispersed across the SEAL units, with the vision thing being one of the rarest traits.

My ability to conceive alternate outcomes was not a blessing in my early years as a SEAL operator. I was pegged as a know-it-all, a weirdo who couldn't stop projecting how things might turn out. I wasn't right all the time, but I was right a lot more than others were. In time, a few officers saw this ability in me and sought my opinion. In the military, it isn't normal for a senior officer to confer with junior officers or, God forbid, enlisted people. Yet over time, as I grew wiser and learned to pick my moments, I began to have influence.

My peers didn't understand why I bothered. Strategy and forward-planning weren't a requirement of the job. Only commanding officers concerned themselves with thinking things out long-term. By the time I received my commission and became a SEAL officer, I was smart enough to know how to communicate my insights. I found that writing those ideas down in a well-constructed thought paper decoupled the message from the messenger. It worked.

At the midpoint of my military career I was assigned to the SEAL's school house command: the Naval Special Warfare Center, or—as we SEALs refer to it—the Center. This unit is famous for being the home of basic SEAL training, the infamous crucible known as the Basic Underwater Demolition/ SEAL course or BUD/S. It is during the early weeks of this long screening process that Hell Week occurs.

Hell Week is a five-day endurance event that pits the students against time, the cold, sleep deprivation, and physical exhaustion, to provide the stimulus required to allow each man to find their own path to understanding. No two students experience Hell Week the same way, and no two students accept or reject the fear, anxiety, and pain created by the highly choreographed and monitored experiment in quite the same manner either. While BUD/S is the centerpiece of the Center, there are a myriad of other courses taught there, too. Basic mini-submarine training, basic and advanced military skydiving known as free fall, junior and senior officer leadership courses, and special high-speed boat training, to name a few.

When I arrived in Coronado, California, in 1990 for my tour of duty at the Center, I was assigned to the land warfare phase of BUD/S. In this nine-week block of the course, students learned how to shoot rifles, pistols, and machine guns. They learned how to use a map and compass to navigate terrain. They also learned basic combat tactics and how to blow things up with demolitions.

I wasn't happy with my new orders. I'd been selected for a special unit conducting combat operations in Panama and expected orders to go there. Instead, I was wet nursing eighteen- to twenty-three-year-old kids. The other reason I wasn't happy was Saddam Hussein. The day I checked into the Center was the very same day Iraq's tyrant invaded Kuwait, starting what was to become the First Gulf War, also known as Operation Desert Storm.

I watched the television news that night and felt immensely sorry for myself. There was no doubt in my mind that SEALs were going to war, and the Center wasn't in the business of going to war. It was a school, and I was going to watch from the sidelines. The next day I went through the long administrative check-in process. Everybody was fired up. We were going to kick Saddam's butt, and there would be loads of special operations missions to boot. The west coast SEAL teams were lined up on the beach to the north and south of the Center. We could see the buzz of excited activity in their adjacent compounds. It made it worse to be so close but left out of the energy flow happening all around us.

In the Navy, officers attend a morning planning event each

day, referred to as "Officer's Call." All the officers gather and listen to the commanding officer (always addressed as "Captain," regardless of actual Navy rank) and the second in command (the Executive Officer or XO for short) communicate their thoughts, musings, and specific directions for the rest of us to act on.

My first Officer's Call at the Center was on the morning of my third day. I was a new lieutenant, and therefore I was there to listen, not pontificate or add my insights. In those days, the SEALs were evenly divided by location. Half in Coronado, California, and half in Virginia Beach, Virginia. There had been little crossover in the years prior to my arrival in 1990, so I knew only one or two men in the room at my first Officer's Call. As you can expect, regardless of the captain's intended agenda, all focus was on the coming war in the Middle East.

Our captain was a tall, impressive officer with combat experience in Vietnam. He was smart, too, and I mean *smart*. His most recent assignment before assuming command of the Center was in the White House, working as an assistant national security advisor. I didn't know it at the time, but he was on the short list to become our next SEAL Admiral. I could see his wisdom and poise demonstrated in that very first Officer's Call.

He listened politely for a few minutes as the gaggle fired questions like, "Are they going to shut down the Center to draw manpower to the operational units?" and "Can we volunteer to be reassigned to a SEAL team for the duration of the conflict?" This cacophony went on for quite a while.

Eventually, the captain raised his hand and the room quieted down. He calmly explained that the Center would continue its mission, uninterrupted, as it had during the entire Vietnam War, Grenada, and Panama. He focused our attention on selecting and training the SEALs of the future, so when their time came to go into battle, they would be ready. He said this was our high purpose and looked around the room inviting a rebuttal.

There was only silence. There would be no transfers either. That wasn't going to be entirely true.

When the meeting broke up, the captain and the XO asked me to hang back. They also delayed the departure of a short, cranky warrant officer. We'll call him George. The two of us sat back down and waited politely to find out what was going on. The captain explained that the Center had received orders that the two of us were to be redirected for a specific purpose. That purpose was to overhaul the land warfare phase of the BUD/S course.

What he said next surprised and shocked us both. He told us the general in charge of the United Special Operations Command (SOCOM) in Tampa Bay, Florida, had indicated through his chief of staff that the commanding general was concerned about "Navy men" running around playing infantry ashore. It was his intent, when time allowed, to send an assessment team to Coronado to determine if the land warfare training at BUD/S should be taken over and led by seasoned Army instructors, specifically with Army Ranger school credentials. There was more. The threat of this takeover didn't stop at BUD/S. They were going to take a hard look at the SEAL teams, too.

George and I sat and continued to listen in stunned silence. The captain explained that we'd been chosen by the east and west coast SEAL teams to protect the BUD/S course. We were to create a plan to clean things up, identify any weak areas the Army assessment team might find, and correct them before they got the chance. We were being given complete freedom to act.

The rub was time. He indicated that the war would delay things, but not for long. We might have three to four months at most to prepare. George and I mumbled that we'd do our best and left the conference room. What I didn't know at that moment was that I'd just observed strategy for the first time, or, more precisely, the clash of two military strategies. I couldn't see how George and I could stop the intentions of a four-star general, but we were going to try.

It took several weeks to redesign one third of the BUD/S course and a few more months to set those changes in motion. As expected, when the Gulf War ended a year later, the folks in Tampa sent out a two-man assessment team, both Army Special Forces operators, Green Berets. Our new program was operating at full speed, and it took a week for the two evaluators to realize we were doing land warfare close to, if not consistent with, US Army standards and methods. The pressure was off; and because of this successful process, I was tapped for a collateral assignment at the Center.

Around the time I arrived in 1990, our admiral established a Strategy and Tactics Group at the Center, staffing the idea with two SEAL officers. Their mission was to assess the current Navy and SOCOM strategies, then work to ensure our Special Warfare strategy was aligned with them coherently. That work meant evaluating every plan, mission, task, and subtask, wherever the Navy and SOCOM thought SEALs should be used around the world. I was the third addition to the group.

While I had a day job as the officer in charge of the land warfare phase of BUD/S, I was expected to take homework with me to the training sites and help work through the tall stack of strategy assessment work. I was not trained to perform in this role. The other two officers were more senior and experienced, and they were highly intelligent—no doubt the reason our admiral chose them to stand up the group. I asked a lot of questions, listened, and began learning.

I didn't see the utility or the point of the strategy review exercise. I was an operator, a leader at the level of mission execution. I steadily took on more and more tasks and transitioned from a gopher and researcher to a contributor to ideas and the way forward. For eighteen months, I played a small part in the early shaping of how SEALs would be used and deployed for the next decade; and yet, at the time, I didn't see or appreciate the value of this group's work product.

A few years later, as I was leaving the service, I finally saw the value of smart, insightful strategy development and the lasting positive effect of that early strategy work at the Center. Military services were constantly jostling for position, like commercial business rivals. Competition was fierce, yet subtle. Every cutting-edge role or mission had big dollars attached, and those dollars drove strategic planning and action within the US defense structure.

This wasn't the grand military strategy I'd read about in history books. It wasn't about a clash of nations or armies and navies. No, it wasn't one of those classic definitions. Instead, it was a good old-fashioned market share struggle between the services; and within those services, it continues to this day.

Where business is concerned, my process of learning the direct, functional relationship between strategy and success began when working as a financial advisor at Legg Mason Wood Walker, a process which continued when I joined United Bank of Switzerland or UBS as a portfolio manager two years later. My seven plus years in the investment world required a keen awareness and understanding of strategic planning as a key factor when making intelligent investment recommendations for my clients.

Curiously, I found that writing down strategy was perceived merely as an administrative requirement at most publicly traded companies, checking the regulatory and traditional boxes of compliance sufficient to make lenders and shareholders comfortable. The corporate annual reports all looked eerily familiar, a common template to cover the bases. Little inspiration or aspiration showed.

As a professional investor, this lack of clarity and vision was frustrating. An analysis of a company's stock should begin with a look at the surrounding influences on the economy, the market or industry, the market sector the company operates within, and a study of key competitors. The same collection of logical inputs you would hope to see addressed in a well-written business strategy.

Maybe it was smart to leave things vague. Who wants the opposition to know your strategic intent in detail? However, over time it became apparent to me that there generally wasn't a better strategic action plan, a vision statement and guide to the company's future, for internal management use. Often, these senior and mid-level leaders were left reading the same administrative document produced for public and external stakeholder consumption. It puzzled me then and it still does today.

However, there were diamonds here and there. Companies whose strategies directly contributed to their long-term success. Berkshire Hathaway, Netflix, and Facebook, to name a few. These companies, and many others, crafted a simple and straightforward message to their customers, competitors, and their employees. The simpler the better in my observation. Persistently focusing on the endgame, target performance, vision, and goals marked these companies as different and, eventually, extraordinarily successful.

I also sensed a conflict between strategy and execution in most publicly traded American businesses, and later the same thing in venture capital and companies backed by private equity. This conflict was hard to detect twenty years ago, but today it is clear for all to see. Short-term stock, or valuation gratification, trumps strategy.

The art and science of visionary planning has been usurped by the art and science of performance optimization. The latter's focus on business minutia and short-term "key performance indicators," or KPIs, has institutionalized short-range leadership and relegated strategy to the back shelf, a compliance requirement without true leverage over day-to-day or ongoing business execution.

Imagine a perfectly operated railroad that led to nowhere of value, and you can begin to see the problem. In recent years, this hyper-focus on the present and the past has been labeled "optimization." The word appropriately defines the actions a vast majority of leaders and managers perform every day. So, what's the downside of optimization? Likely the worst thing is opportunity lost on a grand scale or being blind to threats looming just over the horizon. Also, all the precious resources expended going in the wrong direction and the inevitable painful and expensive reaction when leaders realize short-term focus led them into an ambush or past a pot of gold.

If you read my first book, you are aware I'm not afraid to break a few eggs to make an omelet. Clear and coherent strategy, coupled with nimble and insightful leadership, works. In a crazy world, where pandemics rewrite business history and technology destroys as many companies as it creates, optimization for optimization's sake is a recipe for failure. Investment in people, systems, and building a new version of the future cannot be accomplished if "investment" is a dirty word.

Investment is the opposite of optimization, and as such it is difficult in an optimization-driven organization to convince anyone to stop and think about the future, let alone spend capital on that future. This mindset, I believe, has been driven by the technology that provides us with big data and the means to analyze that big data.

I'm all for using these tools to understand what just happened, how to avoid the bad and reinforce the good going forward. If you are in a stagnant industry, or one that marginally grows at less than one to two percent per year, optimization and the analytics derived from that effort may be useful to project your reality forward. If you are not, this linear projection of expected outcomes will be challenged or rendered moot by a wide range of external drivers of change.

In the military, we say it's great to have a plan, but never forget the other guy has a plan, too. A more enlightened, visionary competitor is already pulling ahead, redefining the deliverables and value proposition, and disrupting your customer base. *Be Visionary, Strategic Leadership in the Age of Optimization* addresses the justifications for strategic thinking, planning, and leading to create long-term success. I will illuminate the positive impacts of operating under a clear strategy, supported by a coherent and nimble operations plan. I will demonstrate the proper use of optimization but also extoll the virtues of messy growth as a means to a legitimate end.

As a visionary leader, you need to stop generating strategy for strategy's sake and craft a path that is both resilient and provides a beacon to lead your organization to new and greater opportunities, as well as through the dark times that any business inevitably experiences. If you've read my first book, *Be Nimble, How the Navy SEAL Mindset Wins on the Battlefield and in Business*, you know my emphasis is on personal discipline, behavior, and the humbling responsibility of leading others.

This book will be anchored firmly to a similar mindset. The leadership skills and knowledge I gained in the SEALs greatly influenced my leadership strategies, operational planning, and execution over the next two decades in business. There are plenty of examples that will illustrate how I go about seeking wisdom, contrary information, and how I eventually convert insight into intuition, intuition into vision, and vision into coherent strategy. Hold on tight—it's time to be visionary!

Chapter Two

Doing What's Right—Leadership Ethics

It takes 20 years to build a reputation and five minutes to ruin it. If you think about that, you'll do things differently.
Warren Buffet

At the end of the day, I'm a simple Nebraska boy at heart. I grew up in simpler times, raised by parents who grew up during the Great Depression in Iowa. They experienced World War II by participating in community rubber and tin drives, baking goodies for the soldiers and sailors, and always, through it all, working. My mom and dad didn't have a choice regarding work ethic or community service. It was what America stood for in the early and mid-twentieth century. As their children, my brother, sister, and I didn't have a choice either.

Much has been written about the so-called Baby Boomer generation, and alas, most of it is accurate ... the good and the bad. In this chapter on leadership ethics, I want to focus on the good parts (of course!). As self-serving as this sounds, it is relevant to my personal code of conduct. A code that will resonate throughout this book.

The two elements that mark my generation—work ethic and community spirit—feel a little corny in hindsight, as I sit here typing. They have been under assault, their definitions twisted and distorted until references to them have become meaningless. But when I was growing up, there was no confusion on these themes. It was a way of life.

My parents welcomed new neighbors and wrote regular letters to those who moved away. My mom was a proud member of a group called "Welcome Wagon." This group organized formal outreach to new arrivals, delivering food, drink, maps, guides to stores, any bit on information they thought might be useful. This included a typed list of names and phone numbers, babysitters in the neighborhood, which kids mowed yards or could run errands. Hard to believe it now, but this was a duty and an honor for these women.

The men in my world formed an informal mutual support system. Everybody knew how to fix everything. Their fathers had made sure of that. Tools, expertise, and muscle were lent to neighbors with a smile and always a little advice on how to do the task right. During holidays, there were patriotic block parties; and during tragedy, everyone came together to support the afflicted neighbor.

I watched this world and was directed, under pain of a long and imaginative list of punishments, to conform, to support, and to prepare for the day I would be a member in good standing in the community. Boys of my generation remember the golden rule of the time: "If you borrow something from somebody, bring it back to them in better shape than it was when they gave it to you." In practice, this was simple. Don't borrow a shovel and return it dirty. Don't return a borrowed lawn mower without using a file to resharpen the blades.

I think you get the point. Why does this matter? It matters because being a good leader requires both work ethic and a sense of community, a commitment to more than self. Regardless of where and when you learned these principles, they *are* principles.

My dad was a punctual man. Yes, I'm a stickler for punctuality also. His generation believed it was a grave insult to waste another person's time and being late wasted time. He didn't have to like or respect the person to follow this dictate. It was just the way he rolled. It also was the way all the dads rolled, and as I soon learned, the way all my bosses rolled.

Being late, even once, was grounds for being fired, seriously. Another mandate was referred to as "a full day's work." This didn't always refer to an eight-hour day, but instead meant that you worked straight through the job, project, task, or time frame without stopping unless told to.

Kids, and teens in general, don't do well with this concept. I didn't either. After losing a few lucrative neighborhood projects and at least one real job, I adapted and grudgingly followed the mandate. Looking back, it seems right to have worked for every minute I was paid to work. A simple concept, but it's a core element of what we call work ethic.

The ethical element is a personal decision. It may feel like a one-sided deal, but these basic rules of work collectively align with the legal definition of a valid contract. Value exchanged between two willing and competent parties. It's been the value chain of human commerce for thousands of years. Labor in exchange for money, money in exchange for food and shelter.

Free Will

As a teenager, I was as rebellious as the next kid. I lived in America, land of the free and home of the brave; but if I screwed up (and in those days the list of potential infractions was long and detailed), my freedom was taken away. Being grounded was a favorite way to reinforce personal, family, and social rules of order. Behavior was on parade twenty-four hours a day, seven days a week. Every one of those oh-so-friendly neighbors were authorized to catch you doing something wrong and, in some cases, even allowed to mete out community punishment.

The struggle was psychological more than physical. Acting out was a fast way to get grounded, *longer*. Fighting the verdict was just plain stupid. In this America, every home could be converted to a gulag with a word. Yet, my spirit yearned to break free, and I learned my peers felt the same way. We spent countless hours discussing escape plans. The destinations were silly fantasies, and the outcomes were always rewarding. Our parents would feel the pain of departure, and we'd be living it up in a big city doing something really cool for a lot of money. No more chores, no more rules, and no more punishment. One by one we goaded each other until one or more of us did the heroic deed: we ran away.

Running away, I now see, was like a bad SEAL mission. Always poorly planned, executed without sufficient supplies, usually a bad map, and always a lack of cold weather gear. When I finally decided to express my free will and make the move, I was angry; and being angry, I left on impulse. I bolted from the back of the house carrying a dark green Easter basket filled with food stolen from the kitchen (That's right. In my day, kids needed permission to take food out of the cupboard or refrigerator. Rule ninety-seven, I think). I had about two dollars in loose change from finding old Coke bottles and returning them to the grocery store for ten cents each, all any eleven-year-old needed to start out in the world.

I walked the two miles to the store, spent all my money on candy (why not? I was a free man) before deciding to go to a local farmer's field to chew on my candy and contemplate my next move. My next move was to freeze to death. The day ended; and as the warming rays of the sun disappeared below the horizon, the temperature dropped. My master plan hadn't anticipated this possibility, so I sat there in a cotton shirt under a mulberry tree and began to shake.

The front door to my house was locked when I returned. I rang the doorbell. I'd determined that the worst punishment my dad might deliver was better than suffering the bitter cold. He opened the door, looked down at me, and said, "Your dinner is cold. Your mother is waiting for you in the kitchen." That was it! My first experiment in free will, bucking the rules, and no punishment!

I figured out much later in life that my dad may have known I'd suffered significantly already. Emotionally and physically. As I sat in the kitchen eating my dinner and sipping the hot chocolate my mom insisted I consume, I concluded that free will was dangerous. I knew instinctively that I must learn more, become wiser, if I was going to test its awesome power ever again.

My straightforward, values-based upbringing served to guide me through most of the moral and ethical dilemmas I faced as a teenager. I did know right from wrong, and I understood the world would be a better place if everyone lived by the Golden Rule: always treat others as you would have them treat you. I was loyal in a social sort of way. Loyal to my family, loyal to my closest friends, and I guess loyal (or obedient) to my employers.

I was one of those "good kids," who spent most of his time working one or two jobs (there's that work ethic thing again) and maintaining the list of family chores and duties. I did take risks and ran around with a few kids who stretched my horizons, but I wasn't a juvenile delinquent. The label "high-risk teens" were given by parents at the time. I didn't know it then, but my personal sense of duty and commitment at the end of high school was shallow, weak, and barely defined. That was about to change.

Military Discipline

I joined the United States Navy through an early entry program. This meant that I signed up and swore an oath to defend the nation, all while I was in high school and almost a year away from attending military boot camp. Once I did the deed, I didn't see or hear a peep from the Navy until a month before high school graduation. All at once I was riding the storm. Testing, physicals, background checks, and lots of forms. I was scheduled for my boot camp date, and before I knew it, I was getting my long, shoulder-length hair shaved off, along with hundreds of other stunned young men. I was in the Navy now!

Why is this part of my life important? Well for one, I learned a strict form of discipline in the Navy, and I learned it right up front in boot camp. The second reason was context. The discipline I learned that we all learned, was aimed at making the community of sailors better, not the individual. It was all about "we" and not "me."

This process is the same for all service boot camps. As military professionals, we are expected to be ready to die for our country, and, even more intimately, be willing to die for each other. This is a selfless form of discipline, and a concept that many people who do not share a military upbringing have a difficult time understanding. Sailors, soldiers, Marines, everyone in uniform, the reason they are there is to serve others and each other. To understand my brand of strategic thinking, planning, and operating, it is important to understand the foundation my brand is built on.

After Navy boot camp, I went to RADAR operator and air traffic control school. This was a crazy difficult challenge for me and all the other students. We first learned basic electronics, so we could fix and maintain the equipment we'd be learning to operate. Then we learned how to track ships and planes, both friendly and hostile. Always being told we were the first line of defense for hundreds, maybe thousands of sailors who depended on our vigilance.

One error, one lapse in concentration, could mean disaster. It was a lot for a seventeen-year-old to absorb. I buckled down, matured, and accepted the charge. No one would sneak up on the fleet when I was on watch. While RADAR school taught me mental discipline, it also reinforced the collective mission concept in the Navy to serve and protect the country, initially instilled in me during boot camp. My next challenge was discipline on a whole new level.

I reported to BUD/S at the ripe old age of eighteen. I was one hundred and twenty-five pounds soaking wet, and thanks to great genes, I looked twelve years old (a curse until I passed the age of forty). The SEAL training experience was the opposite of boot camp. Sure, there were rules, lots of them. We marched and ran in formations just like in boot camp, but it was different.

The point of BUD/S wasn't to groom you, train you, or motivate you to become a SEAL. The purpose of the grueling twenty-six weeks was for you to find your inner SEAL. It was all psychological. The physical torture, the lack of sleep, the cold water, they were all environmental inputs to elicit a psychological state of mind. Each BUD/S student was to decide to stay, move forward, or quit. The struggle was between the voices in your mind, not with the SEAL instructors.

Even today, when I watch documentaries about the SEALs and the BUD/S course, the commentators get it wrong. They show endless reels of desperate young men struggling physically to perform simple tasks like moving a heavy log or boat from one spot to another. They emphasize these visuals and declare the mystery solved.

Although it may seem like SEALs are tough because they were beat up and tested to the extreme at BUD/S, the truth is more difficult to stuff into a sound bite, hard to capture with a camera. The truth is this: a SEAL is what is left over after all the voices in your head make the decision to commit. That commitment is to yourself, an internal oath of sorts to never, ever, let your teammates down.

Always strive to improve professionally so your value to the team increases over time. After BUD/S, no one gave us lectures about discipline, duty, and responsibility. Being a SEAL already encompassed all those values and more.

Don't get me wrong. Other services have elite programs much like the SEALs, and they too find the diamonds hidden in the piles of coal. Time in uniform also gels one's sense of obligatory discipline into a selfless, internalized character trait. As this behavior gets stronger, people in uniform begin to cross the line from discipline to honor. A code of expected general conduct that after a few years in the service feels a part of everyone.

This also is about the time when military professionals begin to completely assimilate into this unique culture. A culture comprised of dedicated experts all pulling together to make it work, whatever "it" may be. People willing to sacrifice—yes, sacrifice—what they have, including their lives, for a greater good, for other citizens they will never meet. It is this fully formed merger of discipline, duty, honor, and culture that is so greatly missed by military veterans when they leave the service and attempt to enter the outside world.

I've tried to develop these same trends, traits, and cultural norms in every organization I've led since retiring after twenty years in the Navy SEALs. I'm convinced the level of effort is worth the results. Companies—small, medium, and large—are collections of people. People who for the most part were raised to be considerate, forgiving, and attentive.

The general level of intelligence and learning capacity also has improved steadily. I am convinced that it is easier than ever before to coach, mentor, and lead professionals toward a strategic goal, if they have commonality of purpose and vision. I've seen both basic discipline and the higher order, a sense of honor, swell up and blossom over time in a commercial enterprise. Each employee looking out for the greater good, convinced that by serving the team, department, division, company, or corporation, they also will be served personally through collective success.

Honor, ethics, honesty, discipline—these are all allies in the pursuit of exceptional outcomes. Tony Dungy, a successful NFL coach and leader, said in his 2011 book *Uncommon*, "Integrity is what you do when no one is watching." I'd add the other characteristics, behaviors, and traits noted in this chapter to Tony Dungy's definition of integrity. Leaders require a core sense of right and wrong. A value system that communicates, through behavior, that they are focused on the greater good and prepared to lift all involved to attain that betterment. Call it a philosophy, a code. Whatever you name it, it is a key ingredient for successfully leading strategic change.

So, now I've told you how my early childhood and military experience influenced and shaped my approach to leadership ethics. It works for me. I've continued to evolve, and from time to time, I stumble, too. Nobody's perfect, especially me. In fact, from my perspective, the more you learn, grow professionally, and take business risks, the more you are faced with fresh dilemmas that don't fit an old solution...or worse, lie in a gray area between what is clearly good and right and what is not.

By now you will have lived your own unique experiences. Some pertain to the subject of this chapter and others do not. I suggest you sit down and take inventory of your value system, first as a person and then as a business leader. Do you sway and wiggle when faced with ethical challenges? Or do you see things as clear and well-defined? This is a situation we, as leaders, find ourselves in occasionally.

For example, I've been faced with the choice to reduce the labor force to meet a financial target or live with the failure and take the heat. This happens across all industries and is a key theme of this book. When is tactical expediency and operational optimization detrimental to the long-term success of the business? If we suppose I was an ethical and honorable leader in this situation, why would I not serve the short-range goal of hitting a number? What's the upside of retaining the staff and facing the imminent failure head-on? By now I hope you know which path I chose.

Attracting, vetting, and retaining top talent is the bane of every organization and a pain point every business leader faces almost daily. Replacing these rare hires (ones that meet all your needs and specifications) can be costly, both in time and money. To cycle back and forth from hiring people to firing people may serve a short-term objective, but it is dangerously short-sighted and reactionary. Being strategic, being visionary, and planning accordingly takes patience and a stiff resolve to weather the little storms on the way to the big payoff on the horizon.

A vision, supported by strategic thought, is like a road map. I have tried to cut corners navigating austere terrain, desert, swamps, mountains, and dense forests. It never works. The plan indicates that cutting across, ignoring the prudent and well-thought-out course, will save time. I have learned that the navigation plan is so important that it may be the second most critical element of success, after the application of visionary and strategic leadership. By the time I began leading companies instead of Navy SEALs, I'd embraced the discipline of planning out the future. I don't cheat across what appears to be easy "terrain" just to speed up the timeline or achieve a portion of my business objectives.

In the following chapters, we'll discuss how to develop a blueprint, how to lead the strategic planning process, and how to develop an operational navigation plan to achieve your vision. For now, it's important for you to center yourself and inventory your values (ethics, moral code, integrity, honor, and so on), as they pertain to strategic business leadership.

As always, note your strengths and your weaknesses. Make a list of these and create a plan to continue what you do well and improve what you do not. We are all human, so don't be too rough on yourself. We're really talking about the basics here. Would you throw a peer under the bus to save your job? Or to get a promotion? Would you lay off ten employees to make your boss happy? Even if by doing so it made you and your business weaker, even vulnerable? Like I said, basic rules of right and wrong are a sufficient measure to answer these simple questions.

The behaviors discussed in this chapter are important at every level of leadership and in all types of organizations: public, non-profit, and for-profit alike. The very essence of being visionary is aspirational, inspirational, and invigorating.

These are all positive points of focus and should be pursued with ethical and moral vigor. A strategic leader can change the world by example. You can change the world, too!

Develop an approach that will allow you to communicate the art of the possible to those eager to embrace your master plan and lift their spirits during even the worst of times—especially during the worst of times! The rest of this book will address the factors that conspire to trip you up on your way to the pot of gold at the end of your vision and will provide you with insights and guidance to help overcome these temporary obstacles on your way to the big wins. Let's get started!

Chapter Three

Self-Discipline

In life, you have three choices. Give up, give in, or give it your all.
Charleston Parker

It took several years as a young adult to establish my discipline system. Like most of you, I had the restraint of others—my parents, teachers, coaches, and older family members—imposed on me. Maybe you also had to embrace the parameters of a religious belief. The point is that you were not living your life based on your own set of objectives, your own drive to accomplish tasks, to be productive, or to be happy. The discipline of youth is an external influence on your behavior, not a core operating system.

In the previous two chapters, you learned a little about my upbringing and the forces that shaped and influenced me as a young man. I thought it important to reflect on this so you might better understand my leadership journey, and more specifically, how that quest has progressed over time. I touched on the concept of work ethic as a core behavior; but until I was in my twenties, this behavior was more about compliance than freely exercising an ingrained ethos.

The Self-Driven Leader

There are several attributes I believe help a good leader become a great leader, and self-discipline is one of those qualities. A discipline dictated by a personal code of execution. A personal focus on quality of effort and first-rate outcome. A behavior profile that doesn't rely on outside influences to operate and thrive. Leaders are surrounded by people all the time. Their family, friends, peers, coworkers, subordinates, and their bosses.

Leaders are not alone in the classic sense of that definition; yet they often are isolated in their accountability.

The concept of personal accountability goes hand-in-hand with what I've touched on so far. Accountability is knowing that the responsibility to perform, to execute, is yours; and if you own the company, yours alone. It is this accountability that separates leaders from everyone else. Your spouse, children, next-door neighbor, the receptionist, the junior salesperson, middle management—none of these people are accountable for leading at your level, for doing what you must do to be successful. Leadership isn't a solo act, but the kind of discipline a leader requires to survive and flourish is certainly an internally driven behavior.

Navy SEALs do not come disciplined and highly focused fresh from the box. Like all people, SEALs begin with a basic awareness of what is expected from them, but they don't truly grasp the depth of commitment that being a successful SEAL will demand from them. This appreciation grows slowly. It is the responsibility of every SEAL to help the team get stronger, especially the more seasoned and senior-enlisted SEALs. They are specifically tasked with this duty to groom, challenge, and mold the younger SEALs. Teaching self-discipline is also a team effort.

Failing to do what others expect you to do is grounds for ribbing, punishment, or social indifference. Being a respected member of the team becomes the motivating factor that converts young men in their early twenties into self-driven professionals. As a result, very few direct orders are ever issued in the SEAL teams.

The power of group expectations is enough to subtly force the behavior-change in each individual, and eventually the internalization of that change converts external obedience into a professional core attribute. It takes three to four years for an enlisted SEAL to assume the first rung on the leadership ladder. Another ten to fifteen to achieve the highest rank. Officers begin as leaders, but they too must evolve and learn how to become a self-disciplined professional.

Trust, in leadership and in each other, is the glue that binds SEALs so tightly together as a unit. This trust is primarily based on a shared sense of discipline and commitment to each other. Then to the mission. For SEALs, this makes perfect sense. The mission is the simple part if everyone is of one mind and spirit. Easy day.

Discipline and Strategy

If strategy is both a vision and a plan to achieve that vision, I'll submit to you that leadership discipline, more precisely *self-discipline,* is a critical requirement for you to succeed on your quest. Consistency of thought, behavior, and drive are prerequisites to executing and reaching a long-range objective. For example, as I sit here in the dark at five in the morning typing this paragraph, I know I have other options—sleep being one of them. I also know my official day begins at eight in the morning.

As the sun rises, the messages will begin to zip in faster and faster. Emails, texts, calls, and then the inevitable meetings. This will continue for twelve hours until business operations on the west coast of the United States cease at five in the evening. If I didn't make a disciplined effort to write from five to six thirty in the morning, every morning, then I'd never finish a single book, and this is my tenth published work in six years.

Leading strategy is no different. There are always distractions, alternatives, easier paths; and many leaders are diverted by the universe's attempt to confuse and dull a leader's sense of purpose. Most people who follow leaders want calm, tranquility, the status quo. Either they disagree with a strategy, don't see the point of creating a business plan (optimizers fall into this category), or don't want to go through the pain and suffering associated with a strategy.

This last group follows the mantra, "If it ain't broke, don't fix it." Strategic leadership is challenging, but it is far more difficult if you don't have a core system of disciplined behaviors that carry you forward, ever onward, despite the friction and resistance the world throws at you.

I devoted an entire chapter on wellness and health in my first leadership book, *Be Nimble.* I did so because leadership is a high stakes game of stress and uncertainty. Stress can become mentally debilitating, but it has ramifications physically as well. A coherent fitness regimen, a proper diet, and sleeping well combine to make anyone healthier. A leader needs all three to assist in handling stress. This book isn't about exercising, but I suggest you strongly consider starting if you haven't already.

I exercise five to six days a week, and no, my workouts aren't Navy SEAL marathons of pain and suffering. I commit to a solid and productive twenty to twenty-five minutes. It's balanced, achievable, and rewarding. At this point in my life, I just want core strength and agility. I'm not aiming to win a weightlifting event, a triathlon, or any other athletic competition. I do it to stay healthy and clear my mind at least once a day.

Diet is another area that requires self-discipline. My wife and I love food and we're human. I retired from the SEALs weighing in at one hundred and sixty pounds. Since then, I've ballooned up to one hundred ninety-eight pounds, dropped down to one hundred and sixty-two pounds, and finally stabilized for the last five years at one hundred and sixty-eight pounds.

We stock the house with healthy choices and practice intermittent fasting. Of course, I must leave the house every day to run the gauntlet of food choices in the real world, and that makes it hard to be perfect. My son is a highly qualified sports medicine professional, who works with a wide range of personalities, body types, and attitudes.

His rule to address our basic nature is simple. Eighty percent of the time be strong-willed and stick to the plan. This includes exercise, diet, stretching, and sleep. The other twenty percent of the time it's okay to be human, to allow discipline to slip a little. He explains that this is an achievable reality.

Absolute perfection is not.

Sleep rounds out the trifecta of health. I've found over time that my sleep is positively affected by a good diet and exercise. Experts disagree on an exact amount of sleep to aim for, but the range is seven to eight hours. The quality of that sleep is also critical. I suggest doing research on the technology available today to monitor the quality of your sleep so that you can assess what's happening at night.

Your body and mind require restful sleep to function at peak efficiency and effectiveness. A deficit in this area will amplify the negative effects of workplace stress. It is nearly impossible to make good decisions when unhealthy, sleep deprived, and stressed out. You can maintain a lack for a short period (I've done this as a SEAL leader), but it isn't sustainable.

Look for these health issues in your direct reports as well. Pushing tired, burned-out people with underlying health conditions isn't a recipe for success. It is hard to lecture anyone if your house isn't in order. So, if you are following a healthy life plan, great! Continue the discipline as an example to your direct reports and your employees. Only then can you intervene to assist when the team around you is showing signs of poor habits.

Sponsoring wellness programs is beneficial, too. You don't have to go overboard. Stocking the company kitchen with healthy food is a start. Allowing flexible work hours, so people can take advantage of fitness centers, is another. In the end, staying fit and healthy is about personal discipline. It is the foundation upon which rests all your applied leadership skills and knowledge. To be visionary may require you to be healthy, too!

Inspiration Is All Around You

I don't spontaneously arrive at new and exciting views of the future. Most of the time the visionary elements are simply bits and pieces of the internal and external business environment swirling all around me every day. Industry thought leaders, wild entrepreneurs, boards of directors, direct reports in management, and competitors…they all have ideas and opinions.

I listen to them all. Odd comments, weirdly phrased observations, kooky ideas, and many without context or focus. A random series of misaligned insights and confusing conclusions that stimulate my imagination. I jump in and absorb the data flow, and fuzzy patterns begin to form in my mind. I lean into the pattern and seek more information. The more I pursue change, the smarter I begin to feel about what's possible.

The constant search for contrary data and market trends that contradict the normal flow of the day is, you guessed it, a discipline. A personal and professional routine performed daily. Staying in contact with the flow of change that is happening all around us every day takes energy and time. This can be difficult to carve out in practice.

As leaders, we are, by design, required to absorb and evaluate a continuous drumbeat of formal and informal data, presented to us through many reporting streams. This data is usually filtered, and often provided to us with analysis and recommendations. How can you absorb, assess, analyze, judge, and parse all that real-time feedback and still have bandwidth to search for trends and answers about the future? It isn't easy. But the payoff is worth the extra effort.

Group think is a natural side effect of people working together on the same things, in the same ways, repeatedly, without challenging the status quo. It might be said that it is also the result of closed-mindedness. Strategic thinking cannot be parochial; it cannot be derived from breathing the same air day in and day out. Strategic thinking requires intellectual risks. Making it a personal practice as a leader to look outside your normal paradigm is a discipline that will pay dividends. If you want to be visionary, embrace this form of self-discipline and leverage the insights gained from doing so.

As I grow older, I find it harder to be inspired in a big way, but it still happens. About six years ago I read Tim Ferris's book, *The 4-Hour Workweek.* The book was, ironically, about optimizing your life by improving the quality of that life. With quality as the optimization goal, I was hooked.

While Ferris covered a lot of ground, I was inspired by how he addressed time utilization. His exercise looked something like this: take a life inventory of everything you do, all day every day, for seven days. Don't leave anything out. Be honest and accurate about the amount of time you spend on each activity; this is the key to the magic.

Once you've completed that task, start to categorize the activities, and add up the total time per category. Then set that aside and make a list of all the things you want to do that you don't have time to do. Fish, paint, write, travel, sleep, whatever it is, write it down. Once the list is ready, estimate (or research) the amount of time these wish-list activities might take to perform.

The next thing you do is begin to eliminate the unproductive, unsatisfying activities on your life inventory list, giving back the time allotted to create the minutes available to do something more fulfilling. Then swap a positive, rewarding activity for the eliminated activities. What I did was eliminate about two hours a day spent reading or listening to politics and other topics not directly associated with my business focus. I converted those two hours into writing novels and working out. It changed my routine late in life and it works. Read Tim Ferris's book and see if his strategy for improving your life improves your discipline system.

Plan Your Dive—Dive Your Plan

In the SEALs, we have quite a few mottos, quotes, and pithy sayings that inspire, educate, and focus the mind—vital when too much environmental stimulation inhibits mental clarity and decisive action. One such saying is burned into our brains early in training, and it pertains to much more than just diving operations.

We are taught to study enemy harbors in exacting detail. We memorize every pier, quay wall, buoy, and land feature. We also memorize the underwater contours and the terrain on the bottom of the harbor for use in our planning. The target, usually a combat ship, is also studied until we can list its width, draft, number of shafts, screws, and the number of blades on those screws.

Why do you do this? Because when SEALs are sent in to attack an enemy vessel, we do so in the dark, twenty to thirty feet underwater. Our means of propulsion is swimming. We breathe from special systems that recirculate our expelled air, pushing it through a scrubbing filter before mixing it with pure oxygen for us to breathe again. These special devices do not release bubbles: important when you are swimming through an enemy harbor, surrounded by people who want to kill you. Once each pair of SEALs is prepared with their plan, it is scrutinized by their peers and their officers.

When approved, the dive pair walk out to a parking lot and begin rehearsing the dive. Minute-by-minute, turn-by-turn, until they are under the enemy ship. Then they rehearse all the steps to set the explosives in place before walking through their series of navigation legs to exit the harbor.

Under the water, in the dark, and often in the cold, it is easy to start second-guessing your plan. There isn't a road sign, a hill, or a stream to use as a reference point. You must trust your preparation, your plan, and your practiced rehearsal of that plan. This is the origin of the SEAL phrase: plan your dive—dive your plan. Take time to think it all through, plan, and practice, then commit.

Believe in yourself, your training, and your teammates. Leading strategic change is a lot like going on a long, dark combat dive. At times it is difficult to judge your progress. You regularly second-guess your original instincts, your vision, and your plan of action. This is normal; but to win, to reach the prize, you must go beyond normal.

You must apply self-discipline, and in doing so, your goals will be achievable. Put faith in your knowledge that what you are embarking upon is right and essential—then execute. Leadership discipline comes in many forms. Planning discipline is just one more variant.

Communications Discipline

All leaders have observed other leaders communicate their intentions. It starts with parents, then teachers, and eventually organizational leaders. Strategic change cannot be achieved without a tight alignment between goal, message, and *action*. Saying one thing and doing something else won't work. People seek guidance, courage, and inspiration from their leaders; and these inputs are delivered through verbal, written, and physical communication.

I've watched senior leaders wander through the rank and file with a dour look on their face, posture slumped a bit, totally oblivious to the dozens of eyes watching and interpreting this messaging. Are things going wrong? Is there a crisis we haven't heard about yet? I suffer from this from time to time. I think and problem solve constantly. I would walk from place to place, the wheels turning. Forgetting that from the perspective of an outside observer, I appear deeply worried. I know this because people have pointed it out to me. This is the communications discipline I focus on the most.

There's an old joke where a mafia leader is sitting in his restaurant meeting with a local businessman. When the meeting is over, he asks his two bodyguards, Moose and Rocko, to take the businessman out. A few seconds later, the loud report of gunshots can be heard from outside the restaurant.

What you say—precisely what you say—and how you say it, can convey multiple meanings to the recipient of that communication.

Leaders have everyone's attention, and they often forget to

think through the import of the words and themes they choose to use. The way you speak is also a key element of this verbal exchange of information. If your words and body language are spot on, but your tone, volume, or intensity is off, then people take away a different experience than you intended to deliver.

If you take time to observe politicians and CEOs of publicly traded companies when they speak to the media, you will see the difference between those who are polished, poised, and on message and those who are not. The professionalism demonstrated by accomplished communicators may seem staged, but this staging is the direct result of poor communications experiences in their past.

Leaders in positions of power and influence can cause great harm with their words. This applies to all levels of leadership. The consequences may differ by scale, but the damage done by haphazardly presenting information is real at every level of endeavor.

Let Your Vision Pull You Forward

I like to think of strategy as both a noun and a verb. On one hand, it is the shiny object at the end of the rainbow. The end state. On the other hand, it encompasses the collective actions taken every day to attain that goal. It goes without saying (but I'll say it anyway) that being adaptive, flexible, nimble, agile, and courageous are prerequisites for effective leadership at all levels of engagement. Self-discipline is the glue that holds all these behaviors together, so you can perform all the daily operational tasks, live a personal life, and maintain the pace and direction of visionary growth.

Force of will is like self-discipline, and both are needed to accomplish great things, difficult things. The British Special Air Service, or SAS, is one of the premier special operations units in the world today. They trace their origins to World War II and the desert battlefields of North Africa. Their unit motto is

"Who Dares, Wins." Simple and direct. But daring isn't always enough.

As noted in the beginning of this book, I've always had a knack for seeing just over the horizon. It hasn't always been rewarding. Seeing things without being able to effectively influence people to act early, invest early, or prepare early has resulted in many "I told you so" moments.

These core leadership behaviors are even more vital at the strategic level of leadership. They are the pillars upon which your vision rests. Erode this behavioral foundation, and the task of achieving visionary greatness becomes much more difficult. When you feel doubt or are consumed by a thousand minor decisions, it is in this moment that self-discipline is vital to success. Many leaders dream, yet few ever dare to act. And of those few who dare, most falter and even quit before reaching the prize. To have the courage to dare is a start. But to be truly visionary, you must lead a disciplined life!

Chapter Four

Confidence, Charisma, and Humor

Management is about persuading people to do things they do not want to do, while leadership is about inspiring people to do things they never thought they could.
Steve Jobs

Confident people are a joy to be around. They encourage, support, and contribute. They smile a lot and laugh a lot. This attribute is contagious. Confidence inspires us to emulate the positive flow we are observing. If sustained as an element of leadership behavior, confidence can be transformative. The history of warfare is replete with example after example of how a confident leader can turn the tide under the worst of circumstances. There are also plenty of examples of how a sustained level of confident leadership helps the team to win, and win, and win again.

It's important to distinguish confidence from arrogance. Arrogance is a diluted form of confidence without the upside. Arrogant leaders are, by and large, shortsighted. They are self-focused. Their behaviors are more an act than an expression of core values and strength. A confident leader isn't pretending to be stable, mature, poised, and ready to tackle challenges. Their behavior is honest, and as such, potent in a world filled with pretenders.

There are many personality types in leadership, and that's okay. I'm not suggesting a homogenized leader profile is the goal here. Quiet people can be confident, loud people can be confident, emotional people can be confident ... you get where I'm going with this. Being confident as a leader is the goal.

I've worked for many types of confident leaders. The silent

but deadly ones and the screamers. What comes through in both extremes of personality is sincerity. Hard to fake sincerity. People sense it. A competent and confident leader, who is genuinely sincere, is a potent leader. A leader people will follow. A willingness to follow is critical to achieving strategic and visionary success. Inspiration is a lofty word. It conjures up emotional detachment from the status quo and a misty-eyed embrace of the possible.

A leader who inspires others is valuable. This intangible is hard to measure and sometimes even more difficult to explain; but these leaders do exist, and they do move mountains. Study inspirational leaders across all categories of business, politics, and warfare. The common threads are there for you to find and use as a guide to become more inspirational as a leader.

In the late 1980s, SEALs were pushing hard to improve their hostage rescue capabilities. The tactics, tools, and playbook applied for rescuing a hostage was a world away from the traditional lean, jungle-fighter SEAL mission. The new mission was extraordinarily complex and executed with blazing speed. There wasn't an option to walk away until the target looked better; the hostage's life was at stake. It was a modern form of charging a machine gun nest with up to sixty men.

The legacy jungle mission was all about stealth and surprise. Low-tech, little to no radio communications, maximum autonomy with a minimum of warriors. The speed and complexity were challenging our young officers, me included. Jungle warfare was slow-paced, lots of time to think things through. In contrast, hostage rescue required the brain of an air traffic controller and the poise of a high-wire artist.

To deal with this leadership dilemma, the SEAL community decide to create a new leadership designation, Ground Force Commander, or GFC. Those officers capable of juggling all the hostage rescue functions competently would be given this designation, and only those leaders would be assigned to lead the mission force.

Of course, they had to come up with a test to determine who had the unique mix of attributes to calmly manage multiple sniper teams, helicopters, a building or ship assault team or two—with a supporting cast of external reinforcements and intelligence platforms hovering up in the air somewhere. The test was to perform the GFC role (after classroom training) with all the assets and capabilities swirling around the target in real time. No simulations.

The test was expensive to say the least, and just getting it scheduled and organized would challenge the most organized Hollywood director. Each of us would get two opportunities to pass. Unfortunately, I was the first officer up. Lights, camera, action!

I stood there, twenty yards from the five-story target building, running the guidance through my head over and over. The radios started to crackle to life. Sniper team one in position, sniper team two in position, and so on. Then the aircraft began arriving, establishing circular orbits to cover the roads an enemy response might use to counterattack.

Simultaneous with all this setup, the assault teams arrived in two helicopters. One sliding down ropes onto the roof and the other sliding down to arrive at the main entrance. I began to hear the assault team members communicating with each other as they entered the target building and began engaging threats on their way to find the hostage in time.

This all happened in a flash. My prior experience leading assault teams was influencing where my attention was drawn to, and that was my downfall. I didn't clearly hear the extraction helicopter's radio message, providing the code word that meant they were in position awaiting my command to come in and pull everybody out. I mumbled something in response, but kept my brain locked on the progress of the two assault teams.

I was as surprised as everybody when two huge helicopters

landed in front of the entrance to the building. The target was not secure, and the hostage had not been rescued. Before I could tell the helicopters to leave, the words "END EXERCISE! END EXERCISE!" came across the various radio nets. My first test was over, and I had failed miserably. The exercise was at an end.

My SEAL Team Four executive officer was a former enlisted SEAL in Vietnam and had been awarded the Silver Star for rescuing the Governor of Granada and his family during the 1983 US invasion of that island. As I stood there, angry at the helicopters for messing up my test, he came over and took me by the arm, gently walking me away from everyone else.

He calmly explained how my garbled response to the helicopters sounded like the code word to come in and recover everybody. He proceeded to tear my short tenure as GFC apart, pointing out my errors, the chief of which was my getting mesmerized by the play-by-play in the target building as the assault teams searched.

He was a quiet guy. He always had a slight tilt to his mouth, as if any second, he was going to smile. His eyes conveyed the same mirth. This helped but didn't eliminate the sting I was feeling. He told me I had one more chance after the lunch break. He then gave me one simple instruction. He said, "Turn off your radios and let the people do what they're trained to do." This seemed the opposite of being on top of everything, but I wasn't going to argue. I nodded and got something to eat.

The second test was executed flawlessly. I only used the radio to call in the helicopters after the assault teams gave me the thumbs up from the main entrance. I was going to be a GFC, but the experience set my confidence back considerably. What I learned that day was that it wasn't my job to rescue the hostage. It was my job to lead everything and play conductor to the heavily armed orchestra. I also learned why my executive officer was revered as a leader. He was supremely confident, and in the face of chaos, he was calm and reassuring. It was this poise that SEALs respected.

I strived from that day forward to emulate his composure and his way of bringing young leaders down softly, preserving their self-esteem and innate confidence, while delivering a critique of their performance. There are many leadership patterns and profiles that work, but this approach has benefited me to this day. I've found that leading change, especially disruptive visionary change, requires a leader to exude confidence over a long period of struggle.

Charisma Sells

This element of leadership is frustrating to me. It is an intangible with value to be sure. It's that certain something often referred to as flare, attraction, or flamboyance. Whatever you call it, it sells. Actors and politicians know this; leaders should understand its impact, too.

I say charisma is frustrating because I've found it is difficult to train or coach a person to be charismatic. To be truly charismatic, anyway. I've had success helping leaders be less stilted, boring, or unimaginative, but converting a wallflower into Leonardo DiCaprio is a skill that eludes me. Do I have charisma? I guess so, to a point. Not headline-grabbing, leading man charisma, to be sure, but maybe just a little sparkle.

In my case, I started out an introvert. A bookworm who was too undersized in school to be more than a second-string player in sports. I looked so much younger than my age that girls in high school always assumed I was a freshman, even when I graduated. For my first three or four years in the SEAL teams, I was on notice to learn and keep my new guy mouth clamped shut.

It wasn't until I was twenty-five that I began to display a compelling personality while leading. I was more confident; I'd been a SEAL for eight years and was established as a proven professional. I was still small in stature for a SEAL operator, I still looked much younger than my age. But I was able to become more extroverted, allow my sense of humor to show, and was wise enough to appear poised, at least during normal daily activities. I still had a long way to go.

Getting your direct reports to like you by hanging out with them isn't going to help you establish charismatic leadership or gain respect. They may buy you a drink, laugh at your jokes, and act interested in your thoughts; but this doesn't mean they like you. It may be a way to figure you out, to learn how to game your personality, or to see if you are a potential threat to them. If you understand all this, then you participate with both eyes open.

However, many young and inexperienced leaders do not see this social interaction as a risk. The danger here is compromising your responsibility to lead when leading means adjudicating difficult issues, counseling failing performers, or worse, promoting or firing employees. Fearing they will damage relationships, a good percentage of young leaders fall into the trap of over-familiarity. Being liked socially isn't about charisma.

The best way to improve your appeal is to find and then study the habits, behaviors, and communications style of charismatic leaders. Emulate as many traits as you can and practice them regularly. After every opportunity to communicate face-to-face with people, take time to roll back the moment and evaluate your performance. Too crude? Too serious? Too lighthearted?

Note the positives and the negatives and commit to improving. Charisma is the sparkle that, combined with confidence and solid communications skills, empowers a good leader to become a great leader. And it takes a great leader to effectively marshal and apply resources and talent strategically.

Humor and Effective Leadership

I believe a good sense of humor is a great attribute for leaders. It helps you put the stress in perspective and diffuses volatile situations. In the SEALs, humor is the balm that soothes all manner of mental and physical injuries. Laughing about a problem shouldn't be construed as not caring and suppressing an expression of humor in tough times is almost always counterproductive.

Humans laugh when they are happy and when they are nervous. Laughter triggers all sorts of positive chemical activity in the brain that helps to offset the fight-or-flight urges an emergency or big failure can generate. People have a wide range of sensibility when it comes to humor, and I'm not suggesting you buy a joke book and go on tour.

Certain things make some people laugh and others angry. I'm saying see humor in the situation. Smile to convey that you agree it's so bad it's funny. The tension around you will dissipate considerably. Then take a deep breath to signal that's over and it's time to get to work problem solving.

You can tell a lot about your team's state of mind by tuning into humor, or the lack of it, in the workplace. Are your folks somber and serious eight hours a day, five days a week? This isn't natural. Do people relax when you interact with them, but revert to an imposed code of silence when you walk away?

Maybe a subordinate leader is enforcing a stiff work environment policy that is misplaced and subtly destructive. Pay attention. Humor, or the lack thereof, is a key indicator of morale. Morale is a vital element in executing dynamic change, and visionary change is always dynamic and often perceived as threatening. It's your job as a leader to use all the tools at your disposal to holistically address the factors that combine to make strategic growth and change a possibility.

If I were to start all over again, knowing what I know now, I'd make sure my demeanor and communications style was firm but friendly. Open but professional. I'd balance getting to know my people with trying to become their friends. I'd spend more time listening for voice inflections, tone, and body language, seeking clues to the state of individual and group morale. I'd make humor a part of my toolbox to prepare people for struggle or to diffuse high-stress situations.

Since I didn't begin with these insights, I learned the hard way, through experience. As I look back, I realize I've evolved in so many ways, but there are still rough edges that need sanding down. Commit to looking, feeling, and acting confident, and use humor to good effect.

All Leaders Must Align

Just before striking the keys to write this section of chapter three, I was on the phone with a seven-billion-dollar-a-year corporation that was looking for a keynote speaker. As often happens, these calls are a casual yet important first date. Is my message and experience a good fit for the subject or challenge they want me to address?

We resolve this by a series of questions and answers, narrowing it all down until we realize I am or am not a fit, and if they want me to speak. In this particular call, a question led me down the path of subordinate leader buy-in. Strategic buy-in to be exact. Senior leaders are closest to the flame. They see the big picture because it's explained to them. They are expected to execute and meet the objectives according to a strategic timeline. They do this with full awareness of the importance of the objectives and with the top leader's inspirational pitch fresh in their minds. However, below this privileged layer of senior management, the rest of the action agents for visionary change are less informed and less motivated.

I was guilty of this several years ago, when I engineered the acquisition of a small healthcare company. The private equity firm supporting the deal aligned to the strategic purpose of the acquisition and the long-term objective to grow the new entity exponentially. My enthusiasm and vision were contagious (as they must be), but I only directly interacted with my subordinate leaders. These managers nodded their heads at the right time and seemed genuinely fired-up to execute the big, audacious plan; but I realized later they were not turning around and transferring this positive energy and strategic message to their direct reports.

So, for the first year after the acquisition, I gave passionate speeches, applied the personal touch, and expended a lot of enthusiasm for this effort. I did this not only to keep the vision alive, but also to make sure it was understood and enthusiastically supported down to the lowest level of the company. That was not the case. By now we were scaling up. In year two, we went from a handful of employees and medical providers to nearly one hundred.

Messaging was more difficult. I'd missed the golden opportunity in the beginning to ensure every leader in this organization was a passionate convert to the vision bug. As you might expect, once I recognized this shortfall, I personally attempted to rectify the problem. Formal onboarding was adjusted, so new employees would hear the history of the new company and the vision for the future. As often as I could, I gave the vision speech. It was better than nothing, but it wasn't good enough.

What I needed was a leadership team that not only believed in the dream but pitched it to new hires and continued presenting it as a mantra to sustain the vision and purpose in everyone's mind. Another lesson learned for me was that most leaders don't have the vision thing, or they were never developed by others to look into the emptiness of future space and time for insight. They were raised to focus on the problems, worst one first. To optimize for optimization's sake—because incremental, short-term improvements were blessed and praised by their visionless bosses. Seeing this unfold over the first four years of the company's startling growth, I began to form a hypothesis of why this happened in leadership structures and what might be done to correct this cloaked, obstructive behavior.

All leaders must align. In basic SEAL training, they use

linear objects, such as heavy logs, to prove this point with teams of students. To lift, raise, lower, or move the log, they must do so together, perfectly together. Arms and legs in a coordinated dance. To fail is to drop the log. Drop the log and the log work time is increased. Eventually, even the weakest assortment of student personalities figures it out. This log exercise is a metaphor for teamwork and much more.

The physical challenge requires exquisite alignment of arms and legs, without the benefit of rehearsals and practice. Leaders in a business face the same linear challenge when contemplating strategic change. The entire organization must move forward one coordinated step at a time and in the prescribed direction of the visionary goal. All leaders must focus their attention on this long-range process and strive to maintain alignment and morale by communicating and inspiring those reporting to them to believe in the pot of gold at the end of the rainbow.

Firm Yet Flexible

Navy SEALs are hardnosed, tough, and determined. They are also flexible, agile, and innovative. Take time to evaluate your leadership style. What does your behavior convey? What do your spoken and written words convey? Are you tough all the time? Are you so flexible that you can't make a decision stick? Or are you so inflexible that all decisions must come through you first?

This isn't easy, but it is vital if you want to lead change successfully. I would list the strengths and weaknesses and work on the most impactful weakness first. Focus, practice, observe, correct, practice, repeat. Then tackle the next weakness, and so on. At best, it might take a year to change your habits and create new ones. Eventually, it will feel natural to you and to anyone watching and listening to you.

Performing the role of business leader is, at times, just that: a role. This chapter touched on various behaviors, attitudes, aptitudes, and actions that make a manager a leader. A good leader. A visionary leader. It is a difficult role, to be sure. I still struggle to do it all well, even today. Staying balanced, poised, warm, inspirational, reflective, astute, confident, and visionary takes study, practice, and faith in the value that these skills and capabilities will bring to your leadership game.

I stress these things in a business strategy book because strategy is about more than just a plan. To evolve into a visionary leader, these foundational skills are mandatory. Without them, people won't follow; and without followers, you are a leader in name only. You can do this! You must do this! Improve your leadership style and watch the magic begin!

Chapter Five

The Art of Deciding

In any moment of decision, the best thing you can do is the right thing…the worst thing you can do is nothing.
Theodore Roosevelt

I can't count the number of times I was faced with insufficient information, yet, because of my role and responsibility as a leader, I was required to make the call. I'm not referring to legality, morality, or ethics. I'm speaking about functional business decisions. Do we hire more people? Do we pour more investment dollars into an idea? Do we start, buy, or sell a company?

In my experience, the more strategic and far-reaching the decision, the less concrete information and insight is available to me. This chapter is about deciding. From the outside looking in, deciding appears to be a simple exercise of power. You're the boss, you get to decide, so do your thing. If you've been a decision maker, regardless of the level of authority or autonomy you had, then you know deciding is anything but simple.

Nobody wants to make a mistake. Nobody wants to fail. I know I certainly don't. Employees often assume their leaders belong to a protected class and therefore are immune to termination for basic errors and transgressions in the workplace. Even some leaders believe this to be true. If you are a leader with integrity and humility, then you don't hold yourself above the rules or the consequences of failure.

A visionary leader knows that the price of goal stretching, aspirational strategies, and clear-eyed optimism about the future can be failure to achieve. They also understand that this level of failure is impossible to hide or cover up. You may lose your position, your industry credibility, or your feeling of professional competency. These are the risks inherent in making most leadership decisions, but they are amplified when vision-inspired strategy fails.

I made a great call once. I believed we needed to create an in-house financial workflow capability that allowed us to see our medical claims data and optimize net revenue collections. We were being grossly underserved by a small vendor who could not keep up with the parabolic increase in medical procedures, procedures that were converted into insurance claims for our medical group. I saw the problem but spent a year not deciding.

The choices were to find a larger claims processing vendor; to buy a claims processing vendor to create an internal capability; or to build our own capability from scratch. When I finally decided to build our own capability, we had a year left on the vendor contract, so I used this year to design and then build the capability. Here's where I made my second mistake. I decided to make the new capability its own company. A profit center servicing our medical practice group and outside customers.

By the time the new company was created, staffed, and operating, two years had passed since the strategic decision to act had been clear to me. That two-year period was a critical window of opportunity when the medical practice group grew exponentially. We also went from one state to five states and added two new medical specialties. The volume and the new complexity were exciting on one hand, but it was crushing the newly minted medical claims company.

We were incapable of investing in smarter experts and a better cloud-based platform for processing the work. So we did the best we could for two years before pushing most of the effort onto a nationally-recognized technology company that specialized in what we did. This company could easily scale their effort to match our increasing volume and complexity. So, in hindsight, would I act differently, knowing that the medical practice group was about to explode in market share?

Absolutely. I considered this story a failure to decide in time; and as the CEO and primary architect of the failed solution, the buck stopped with me. Sometimes doing the right thing appears easy. I'm here to tell you it is not.

Art or Science?

I'd like to begin by making a clear distinction between being decisive and making decisions. Being decisive is often observed in the moment, real time. There is an obvious choice or choices to make, and the observers know this is the case. They watch the leader, expecting him or her to decide. There is no doubt that a decision of some kind must be made. Strategic decision-making is less supported by a consensus.

Many, including the experts assisting the leader, may not see a need for a decision, especially a strategic one. In this situation, the decision maker finds themselves alone. They see an opportunity or a threat that others do not see. If the leader is decisive and endowed with the authority to act, they may do so without the burden of selling the decision to peers, subordinates, boards, or banks. Most leaders do not have this unilateral authority, so they must become adept in the art of influence.

Since I've been in leadership positions at many levels of authority and autonomy, in and out of uniform, I've always had to apply the art of effective decision-making, influencing rather than ordering agreement in others. Visionary change comes with a long list of disruptive actions, actions that represent threats to the status quo of the organization and its employees. Usually, the more far-reaching and visionary the set of goals are, the scarier they appear to the uninspired. People hope to do their day job well, get a raise, maybe a bonus, and never ever get fired. This is basic human nature: fear of displacement, loss of income, loss of professional relevance, and in a few cases, a loss of positional power and authority.

The art of strategic decision-making lies in understanding

these basic human reactions to change. As a leader, you must pay prerequisite attention to the people who will execute your vision, with an aim to allay anxiety and inspire commitment through logic, empathy, and instilling confidence in your vision. The science of decision-making is a straightforward analysis and planning activity. Create the battle plan, the timelines, and develop the general cost and benefit derived from the new path forward. Once this is in hand, and preferably before presenting the vision to anyone, step back and assume the role of political candidate. Plan your communications campaign: both methods of delivery and messaging.

Your plan may be well-designed, but don't assume a single person will agree to your vision concept. Start humble and honestly think through how to win every "vote." Make a list of the peers, partners, and superiors you must convince and inspire. Develop a communications and influence campaign focused on these critical allies, a persuasive message that will bring them over to your cause. Then do the same thing for the key subordinate leaders reporting to you. Finally, identify (by now with assistance from your new allies) a message for the greater number of affected employees.

Rumors can undermine your narrative and inflame fear, so do all the communicating, at every level, within a few days rather than weeks. Don't let the counter message create a bow wave that dilutes the enthusiasm and positive nature of your core vision and your expectations for better outcomes. Influencing, persuading, convincing, inspiring—these are the tools. Applying these tools in support of your strategic decision to shake things up is an art, for sure.

Collective Reasoning

If you've had an opportunity to read my first book, *Be Nimble,* then you know I spent some time laying out my thoughts regarding group decision-making or crowdsourcing decisions.

I passionately believe that excellence in design, whether service, production, art, or music, is rarely a result of collective compromise. Now I did say excellence. Read about the early days of Apple and the struggle Steve Jobs endured with his naysaying engineers.

The Mac computer, iTunes, the iPhone, and the iPad all were designed as visionary multifunctional devices that would change the world. Their computing power, physical size, usability, and applications were a dream of Jobs'. Mozart and DaVinci didn't gather up their friends and peers and gain consensus. No, they had a creative vision, and, with single-minded purpose, they produced masterpieces. People all around the world are still in awe of their work to this day. Consensus can create and build things that are functional, but things that are truly excellent? Groundbreaking? World-altering?

While I'm not a fan of collective decision-making in business, I am a fan of collective reasoning. Listening to oblique lines of inquiry, odd sources of insight, and, of course, the standard company channels for inspiration and information are prudent and reflect sound judgement. I listen and learn, measure, contemplate; and then when I feel I've absorbed enough to understand the core risks and rewards, I craft a solution for execution.

All the decisions I've made in my professional life have been heavily influenced and guided by the smart people all around me. When my decisions work out, I shower praise on the team that delivered the prize. When they do not, I accept sole responsibility for the failure. Deciding carries with it the obligation to embrace accountability for your actions. In the end, it is your job to make the call and live with that decision.

When I was in the SEALs, we lost more men from training accidents than in combat. We pushed the performance envelope every day, and any SEAL will tell you the intensity and complexity of that training usually exceeded actual combat. I watched officers make calls and suffer through the aftermath when their decisions resulted in men being severely injured or losing their lives. My greatest fear as a leader in combat wasn't for my personal safety; it was the fear that I might make a decision that got one of my men killed or maimed. Leading is hard. Doing it right is even more difficult.

Good leaders soak up the brain power and experience of their team before making decisions. Poor leaders take counsel of their own insights and make the call in a vacuum. Collective insight, reasoning, analysis, and data collection are all great ways to get smarter and make better choices. It is true during day-to-day management and especially true when crafting an audacious vision for change.

It Takes a Team

I've found over the years that few people are strategic in their thinking and even fewer are visionary. It's possible to be both, but that combination of leadership attributes is extremely rare. I separate these two similar but different concepts by level of development. I used Steve Jobs as an example earlier. He wasn't an engineer, he didn't have an MBA, and he didn't create meticulous strategic execution plans for Apple or Pixar. His contribution was visionary insight, an insight that melded style with practical application to create wonderful breakthrough products.

Steve Jobs' second contribution to excellence in visionary execution was unrelenting faith and tenacity. Some leaders can see the future; others, once shown the vision, know how to develop the long-range plan to seize that future. If you are one of the rare leaders skilled in both, then this segment might not apply to you. But for most of us, seeking help to offset a weakness is a smart play.

If you are a visionary, one who is consistently astonished at how your brain pulls together random pieces of information to form a view of what is possible, then it is important to find a skilled strategic planner, or planners. An architect needs an engineer to see his or her concepts come to life. The same holds true for business leaders who have visionary ideas.

I use examples of famous business leaders because we all know their story, but being visionary can be a low-level requirement, too. At the project team, department, and division level, seeing a better long-range path is a critical skill set. If your insight or intuition is screaming that there's a need for big change, but you're not sure how to structure it, then team up with an intelligent planner.

I once was asked to look at an expensive SEAL mini-sub program because I had shown an ability to see things differently. My ignorance was the key. The experts with years of experience were unaware of new uses for the mini-sub and oblivious to why anything new would ever be considered. I did not have this baggage. I was an outsider to the program.

I wrote a thought paper as directed and was astounded when I was sent to a SEAL team, specializing in mini-sub operations, to make the idea in the thought paper a reality. This was the point where I needed all the technical and operational assistance I could get. Writing the thought piece did not convert me into a savvy, fully certified mini-sub pilot and navigator. I leaned heavily on at least fifteen experts to flesh the idea into a concept. Then we took the concept and developed a long-range plan to make the vision a reality.

It took me an hour to write down my opinion, two months to create a plan with a lot of help, five more months to test the plan's assumptions, and another six months to deploy the new capability overseas in real-world conditions. After that six-month deployment, the SEAL teams adopted the proven concept as the new normal for the next twenty years. It took a wide range of expertise and leaders with more experience than me to pull it all together.

I used to wonder why I, a junior officer with no mini-sub

experience, was allowed to lead the process of converting a crazy idea into a valuable new combat capability. I received the answer to that question several years after I retired from the SEAL teams. A SEAL admiral close to the decisions being made at the time told me that my very lack of rank and experience made me the perfect fall guy if my idea flopped. No senior officer was going to risk their career and reputation by having their name associated with the attempt to save the mini-sub program, and I was too junior to have lofty career ambitions.

I was also the most enthusiastic person in the teams when it came to the value of my idea. So, I was set up to both succeed and fail. Thankfully, due to the team of technical people provided to me, we did not fail.

I believe leaders have the responsibility to look to the future and think big thoughts. This may feel odd for you to do, if no one has asked for your strategic input, but it is a leadership responsibility nonetheless. Figure out if you are a visionary, a technical strategist, or a combination of both, by practicing the vision thing. Look at your industry, your company, your niche within your company, and think big thoughts. Write them down. Not as fully developed plans, but as concepts.

Do a What-If exercise. Flesh out the why. If you are comfortable doing so, invite one or two technical experts to look at your concept. Then ask, "How?" My guess is you'll see the restrictive nature of tradition, standard practices, and even formal education come to life to squash your idea. That's okay, it's normal. You need these folks, so start learning how to select optimistic technical partners and practice your influencing skills. If you're not a visionary, find one and become a practical part of that person's vison development and execution.

Bold Thinking Vs Moderation

Decisions attract controversy and emotion. Everybody has an opinion, and they don't have to be leaders to have one about the calls you make. Usually, the more dramatic the situation, the more dramatic the response from the peanut gallery. While the vision can be bold and audacious, the path to attain that goal should reflect milestone achievements that allow the attainment of multiple, progressive wins. These wins provide a stair-step process that feeds into the psychology of project momentum.

I'll go into the application and construction of strategy later in this book, but it is important to commit to a goal worth achieving in the first place. Subtle, incremental adjustments over time feel more comfortable, but this is an example of operational, not strategic thinking. You are simply optimizing your way down a short-range path This is not strategy and certainly not bold, visionary thinking.

Often, if you're thinking bold, beautiful thoughts, those ideas become chiseled away and sanded down by the folks above and below you in the business. Eventually you're looking at a modest adjustment that costs little, accomplishes almost nothing, and threatens no one inside or outside your company.

Choosing to be bold is an important decision. Committing to stand by that bold idea is just as critical. Your position or employment might be at stake by striking out from the pack and anticipating a better future. If you give in and give up or allow the idea to be watered down to a sad, limited version of itself, you may gain relief in the short-term.

However, if you were right, and your vision of the future does become reality, then you'll find yourself a struggling bystander. Coping with a dying company strategy like everyone else. A strategy that was incremental, linear, and modest to the point of safe. The world is changing too rapidly to seek safety to achieve greatness.

So bold wins the day! Be intelligent in the manner of your presentation. Communicate a series of achievable operational goals and objectives that bend the current trajectory toward your bright new future step-by-step. People may still grumble about the value of change and complain about the disruption caused by a change in strategy; but like pearls on a string, your path to success provides managers and employees with a way to experience those changes gradually. Progressively altering what they do every day and providing them with what feels like normal incrementalism, but in fact, leading them in a new strategic direction. Be bold!

Vision and moderation are not compatible concepts. Being bold moves mountains, changes the courses of rivers, and builds mighty nations. There is a reason champions of moderation are nowhere to be found in our history books. Being bold breaks paradigms. Being bold is powerful!

When the Black Swans Fly

There will be times any leader, even the best, is challenged by crisis. Visionary leaders are less likely to be foiled by an unforeseen threat, but it does happen. The black swan concept is applicable here. Modern literature informs us that a black swan is an event that takes us by complete surprise.

The attack on Pearl Harbor in 1941, the 1987 stock market crash, and the attacks on September 11, 2001, are examples of this phenomenon. Of course, Monday morning quarterbacks with the benefit of hindsight eventually connect the dots to show that each of these black swan events were identifiable, if leaders were open-minded about information that didn't fit their world or market view.

The proactive value of visionary leadership is derived from the receptive embrace of insights and information. A willingness to evaluate the collective inputs honestly and objectively. The capacity to be humble, accepting what the data predicts. As a regular leader practice, this approach will, as a rule, inoculate you from most black swans, large and small.

In 1925, Army General Billy Mitchell rationalized how a Pacific adversary could use airplanes, launched from ships, to attack the vulnerable and shallow Pearl Harbor, home of the US Pacific fleet. Billy Mitchell was a visionary; and because of his fantastic vision (the Army could not conceive of any Pacific nation attacking the United States in 1925), he was demoted to colonel and retired from the Army after being court-martialed. Sixteen years later, the Japanese attacked the Hawaiian Islands, using planes launched from ships. Billy Mitchell died just before seeing his prophecy come to life. He was quietly reinstated to general posthumously and had a new bomber named for him.

I have envisioned threats and opportunities during my professional career that often were ignored, even ridiculed. As a leader, I was frustrated by these reactions; but I did what I could within the scope of my authority and resources to prepare anyway.

Once I ascended to the C-suite, I was able to take these inspirations, thoughts, and plans and convert them into actionable business strategy. I lost a lot of good people along the way; most didn't see the future the way I did or were unwilling to think beyond the next few business quarters. I regretted losing them, but I backfilled the gaps with motivated leaders who were galvanized by the prospect of visionary excellence.

My message to you as a leader, or an aspiring leader, is to commit to visionary leadership and try to influence change for the better. Identify risks, threats, and opportunities with an open and inquiring mind. Do what leaders are paid to do, what they are specifically hired to do: make the hard decisions and lead!

Decide to dream, then decide to act. Decide to win through the enthusiastic support of your team, department, division, or company, and keep inspiring and communicating what your vision will deliver until the day it is achieved. Put simply: dream, decide, perform! As a leader, this is your destiny. Fail to embrace it and you will be pushed aside in time. Change is the natural flow of the universe, and business certainly reflects that reality. To sit pat, taking no risks, is a recipe for failure.

Chapter Six

The Three Levels of Management

Without strategy, execution is aimless. Without execution, strategy is useless.
Morris Chang

In the United States military, I was taught there were three distinct levels of leadership engagement. These levels rely upon each other symbiotically. It is hard to do one well without the other to achieve targeted results. These three levels are strategic, operational, and tactical.

When conducting commercial business, I've found applying this stratification of responsibilities and execution to be helpful. I usually modify the last level by labeling it tactical/technical, to incorporate and recognize our heavy dependance on technical execution to succeed at the tactical level of engagement.

The development of strategic goals in the US military often are hampered by the American tradition of requiring symbiotic relationships between our military strategy, our economic strategy, and political/diplomatic strategy…all in support of policies.

This arrangement changes and evolves over time, with emphasis on one, then another, of the three areas of national focus. A dictatorship relies far less on policies and may emphasize the military strategy as the primary focus, with all other national means and resources aligned in support. In a way, businesses are more focused on economic endgames, with all other company or corporate resources in support. Competition isn't actual warfare but supporting strategies and plans must be devised and carried out to understand and unbalance competitors, and, in the end, beat them in the marketplace. Depending on the size of your enterprise, corporate communications—including all aspects of broadcasting your brand, your values, your services, and your products—is akin to diplomacy.

Knowing these three distinct but interconnected levels of business activity and leadership is crucial to streamlining performance and measurement of that performance. As the quote at the beginning of this chapter reveals, leaders who are all hopes and dreams need assistance from those who execute and from those who have their heads down every day, making things happen. Leaders need visionary guidance to make sure they end up someplace worth the effort.

You may feel more comfortable in one level, and that's okay. We all have tendencies to drift to the place that's comfortable. However, if you are an effective leader, you will need to become a student of all three levels to achieve strategic success. Even Christopher Columbus needed a ship and professional crew to fulfill his destiny.

The Strategic Level of Leadership

Let's start with an overview of the strategic level of performance. I've had to explain my strategy, and more often the strategy of the leaders above me in the food chain, more times than I can count. Over the years, I've found the metaphor of travel planning to be an effective way to describe the value of strategy to those who spend their whole professional lives focusing on operational and tactical/technical execution.

A family decides to go on vacation and their goals are to have fun, enjoy the experience, and create happy memories. This family's vacation will be expensive, and they will want to make sure their precious vacation time and money is spent wisely. The travel from their home to the vacation site will undoubtedly require detailed planning, and the family will need to complete multiple tasks and subtasks successfully for the trip to go off without a hitch. What's missing here? That's right: a destination, a final goal.

This family could create the world's best packing list, inspect every bag and suitcase, get the car checked at the repair shop, even practice driving; but without a destination that represents success, this family's preparations are meaningless. They are destined to be all packed up with nowhere to go. By selecting a worthwhile vacation destination, the family makes a strategic choice, aligning their money and their time to the achievement of lifelong memories.

In this example, let's say they choose Disney World. Once the destination has been selected, this family will have countless potential routes they can take to Disney World. They also have a wide range of possible transport options, including a combination of several different modes. If their car breaks down, then they can take a bus, a plane, or rent another car. They can even hitchhike.

As Disney World is the agreed upon objective, the family can travel there directly from their home or, if a storm threatens, take a more circuitous path. If they all know the destination, they will succeed. They do not have to rigidly adhere to the operational and technical elements of this journey to achieve their strategic goal. Flexibility of execution on the way to Disney World may serve them far better than strictly following the plan.

A strategic goal is more powerful if it is simple, self-evident, and aspirational. The simplicity helps you as a visionary leader to communicate a short and memorable message. The organization should be able to understand the strategic goal without requiring coaching and training to see why the goal is valuable and worthy.

Lastly, the goal should represent something difficult but extraordinary. A strategy achieved easily is an example of incremental thinking, not visionary insight. President John F. Kennedy's strategic goal in the early 1960s was to catch up with Russia's early dominance in space. This represented a complex challenge. But Kennedy boiled it down to a simple message: our national strategic aim is to put a man on the moon by the end of this century.

Audacious? You bet. At the time, the Russians were barely scraping the edge of our atmosphere. Popping up into low space in tiny vehicles carrying first dogs and then a human. Kennedy's goal was to land on the closest object in the night sky: the moon. The moon itself became a simple yet powerful symbol of an aspirational American strategy.

Operational Leadership

In warfare, the operational level of thinking, planning, and activity is focused on maneuvers of large capabilities—fleets, air wings, and armies—in support of a short-range operational objective or the strategic goal itself. Operational leadership requires mastery of this large-scale choreography. Logistics, coordination, timing, communications, and other critical categories of performance converge to make a military campaign a success.

In business, operations are often dumbed down to small-scale execution, diminished plans of action. Sales and marketing are the most obvious areas where operational planning and leadership are visible to outsiders. Operational planning can also be applied to product or service design and development, manufacturing expansion and revitalization, and several other key performance categories businesses rely on to excel.

A strategy requires a sound operational program to lay out the milestones to the visionary end state. A few visionary leaders also are gifted in operational thought; but more often, the strategic leader must lean on the abilities of people who thrive at the operational level. As noted in the family vacation example, operational excellence performed in a vacuum is a waste of resources.

We need a goal, an organizational end state that implies

a clear cardinal direction, a heading on our organization's compass. Hand that to a seasoned and competent operational leader and watch the magic happen. If you are that operational leader, right now it's important to see the relationship between strategic goal setting and operational support of your goal. Beyond that, seek to understand how that strategic goal was developed.

Become aware and then expert on strategic thinking yourself. Many talented operational leaders are promoted to top levels in an organization, only to realize they are blind when it comes to evaluating the threats and opportunities that lie on the far horizon.

Strategy answers the question, "Should we be heading this way?" Operations is all about, "How will we get there?" Operational thinking requires stamina, logic, process and systems knowledge, time management skills, communications skills, meticulous management, and three-dimensional situational awareness.

I like operational leadership because it is easy to see the cause and effect of my team's efforts, and my own. Things move and shake in near real time. There is excitement and gratification in meeting a series of attainable objectives on the way to the final prize. None of the wondering and waiting associated with strategic leadership.

The operational leader only has to create a plan and execute that plan. He or she will run into trouble only if they a) drift from the strategic goal or b) operate in an organization that does not have a strategy. This second situation is all too common in midsize and smaller businesses.

A heavy emphasis on operational effectiveness and efficiency, with no regard to the future beyond the next business quarter, is a recipe for disaster. Many large companies suffer from the same lack of direction.

The measure that should be applied to operations is how all

operations align, support, and reinforce the strategy. Operations for operations' sake is seductive. You can feel great about your leadership and, if drifting from the strategic point of the exercise, begin to rationalize and justify the operational decisions you've made up to that point. Of course, a good strategic leader won't let a good operational leader drift.

However, when it does occur, expect the operational leader to react by doubling down on the operational plan, even raising concerns about the original strategic intent. If nothing has truly happened to discredit the strategy, you are observing closed-minded and self-serving behavior focused on preserving traditions, culture, the plan, and the last bad decisions, instead of supporting the vision.

The Technical Level—Where Optimization Lives

This is where the rubber meets the road. Where things are built, fixed, and redesigned. People at this level of engagement are technical experts or on their way to becoming experts. Tasks and subtasks are broken down to micro steps of execution to ensure that execution is precise.

In a restaurant, a chef doesn't throw a meal together, he or she follows a step-by-step plan with identified ingredients and the exact amount of each ingredient to use. Aircraft fabricators don't guess; they follow highly detailed and well-articulated schematics.

Leaders at this level are there to oversee excellence in execution as designed. They have little direct influence on strategy, other than following the big picture operational plans set in motion above their pay grade. It is difficult, but not impossible, for an event at this level of management to derail strategy.

An atrocity conducted by a low-ranking solider can mushroom into international outrage and hasten the end of a strategy to win the hearts and minds of a liberated people. A similarly destructive act by someone in a business also could balloon into a terrible brand-ending event.

Leaders and technical experts working hard at the tactical/technical level require knowledge of the strategic goal. The men and women of NASA in the early 1960s knew their goal was lofty and nearly impossible. But because they understood the engineering challenge of landing a man on the moon, their toil for nearly a decade was inspired.

I believe most operational leaders fail to translate and communicate the organizational strategic vision to their direct reports leading the tactical/technical level. Whenever I sense a blasé atmosphere creeping in, I take the time to speak to everyone I can, personally, face-to-face, to reignite the flame. Then I find their leaders and do the same thing.

As a leader, you should anticipate these disconnects in communications and strive to keep the strategic narrative alive. I locate the operational leaders who report directly to me and let them know, in no uncertain terms, that continuously stoking the aspirational fire is their responsibility. Regardless of which level you are associated with, you can and must be a motivating force, an evangelical messenger spreading the vision across and throughout the organization.

Leading Change at All Three Levels Is Hard

Often, a leader committed to a greater purpose is viewed as cheerleading squad of one. Rarely have I witnessed layers of management passionately echo the CEO or president's long-range themes. Why is this so? My theory is that if there are positive and supportive subordinate leaders, then they are seen by many within the organization as architects of pain, co-conspirators focused more on helping their careers than pushing back on crazy.

Social and peer pressure is often brought to bear on these managers to join the royal opposition to change. They are influenced to work with their non-conforming employee partners to slow down the strategic change effort, if not stop it altogether. The theory is if things are delayed long enough, there's a possibility the CEO will change his mind, move on, or retire.

The majority point of view in companies, especially in the early phases of a new strategy implementation effort, is "Why shake things up?" It's far better to focus on the real role of management, measuring and monitoring the status quo, delivering reports, and keeping it real.

It's key to recognize that adding new imperatives, visionary or not, will add work to everyone's day. You must be mindful of this and strive to offset this extra strain as much as possible. Revisiting projects and their prioritization during the strategic gear-shift is one way to help. Another is to bring in temps, interns, and consultants to spread the old and new task loads around a bit.

Coming up with a new idea or pulling insights from others to create a new vision can be a wonderful experience, or it can be drudgery. Supporting the strategic vision as an operational or tactical/technical leader can also be less than fulfilling. I've observed that it is much easier if outside events or trends, obvious or easily explained, demand immediate and decisive action.

In this case, leaders are expected to act, to behave as leaders. Even with legitimate and undisputable external drivers of change, you will still have problems convincing everyone there's a need to develop a new path to success. It's human nature to abhor change once things are comfortable.

On the other hand, an audacious vision that anticipates what may happen in the future is more difficult to rally around. Your story feels like fantasy, and the strategic threat or opportunity isn't on everyone else's RADAR yet. So, most of the internal stakeholders simply do not believe you.

Another hurdle you may face is that your vision, regardless of its validity or value, will be seen by many as a self-inflicted injury on the corporate body. A disruptive force that isn't necessary. As a leader, a visionary leader, it is your duty to show your subordinate leaders and employees why their desire to avoid risk is shortsighted and misplaced, and why your vision is powerful and appropriate.

Your drumbeat of optimism, this steady diet of positive communications, guiding, cajoling, briefing, and sometimes pleading, is never-ending. As a leader of dynamic change, you and other leaders in the organization must steel yourselves to this task. It must be a part of your daily routine. Checking the pulse, asking people to describe the vision, and confirming their understanding and commitment.

Everyone must know you have not dropped the ball. You are dialed in and driven to reach the strategic objective. Leaders at all three management levels must do this. They must internalize the vision until it becomes a part of them and start singing the new fight song. If the leaders don't do this, nobody else will.

Several years back, I was a vice president of a solidly performing business division. I grew my charges quickly. After assuming leadership, I was able to empower my subordinate directors to achieve surprising results. This made it all the stranger when I was called into the president's office for a discreet chat.

The company had grown into six business entities over a short span of time, rising from two hundred million in revenue a year to three quarters of a billion in less than four years. We were headed in the right direction, but we were a mess institutionally. At least that was the discreet message to me that morning. The president revealed it was time for a major shakeup, a restructuring of the entire cluster of companies; and he wanted me to be the point man for that effort.

I listened patiently to his ideas and those of his boss, the billionaire owner of the corporation, and took mental notes. I left his office with a clear idea of the strategic objective.

Realign the resources and the leadership to prepare for another doubling of our financial performance. I was sworn to secrecy, and for a few weeks I worked on the plan in private. It was odd to do something of this magnitude in a bubble. I was unable to discuss key questions with the other business leaders.

I wasn't an expert in many of the things the other business entities delivered to their markets, so I didn't know if what I was going to propose was stupid, just okay, or brilliant. When I went into the president's office a month after our first discussion, I was as ready as I could be for someone who'd been creating a strategic solution in a vacuum.

I delivered my plan and waited for his response. The president took a few minutes to study my organizational diagrams. I had purposefully noted only titles but no names. When he was finished, he looked up and grinned.

The restructuring plan was approved and my involvement in its development wasn't a secret for long. Within a week, the word was out that I was the architect of the disaster. It was perceived as a disaster because nearly every leader in the corporation was going to be disrupted, promoted, demoted, shifted, or let go.

My masterpiece was spot-on from a logical business point of view, but from a social point of view it lacked empathy derived from greater management participation. Springing the massive reorganization on everybody shocked the place to the foundation. An internal communications plan to roll out the initiative would have greatly reduced the tears and gnashing of teeth. It didn't matter that I also was displaced by my own plan. I lost my business division.

The division I'd spent a year improving and growing was broken into three parts to form new operating units, all under the leadership of other executives. In a twist I didn't see coming, I was placed in charge of business development and marketing for all the business units. I received a raise and a new office.

Up until the day I left, many of my peers resented the strategic changes we made and my role in the design of those changes. The fact that we grew to become a billion-dollar corporation over the next twenty-four months didn't seem to matter. Change is hard, and it is almost always taken personally. Leading change is hard without the social and emotional storm created by discarding the status quo and leaning into the unknown.

Business isn't warfare, but leading change at all three levels of management is more difficult in business than in war. Officers are trained to give orders. Soldiers, sailors, and Marines are trained to take orders. They may disagree with the goals, plans, and actions they're engaged in, but they are paid to salute and execute anyway.

This, of course, isn't the case in the commercial world. Employees and leaders at all levels are not required to salute and quietly obey. They may choose not to charge the hill, or once in possession, stay on that captured piece of real estate. Leading businesses, of all sizes and shapes, is an intellectual, physical, professional, and emotional challenge.

Shaping the future can be lonely and frustrating, and that's why so few leaders take a deep breath and think big. We are all social creatures, and we all have our own fear of failure. Strategic change is hard. You must believe change is needed and then inspire those around and beneath you to believe, too.

Chapter Seven

Strategic Awareness

The only thing worse than being blind is having sight but no vision.
Helen Keller

When the front, or bow, of a boat moves through the water, it pushes the water in front of it, creating a bow wave. I like to think of trends as bow waves. Small and large changes happening all around us, initiated by an effect we may or may not understand. All trends start, flourish, and end, replaced by new trends. Trends are captured and leveraged by people with their eyes open and an ear to the ground.

In the fashion, music, and entertainment industries, it pays to be able to read the tea leaves and act in time to take advantage of the new trend before it fades away. Trends are an expression of collective human behavior, rising slowly until reaching a tipping point, when the behavior becomes mainstream. Leaders who understand these phenomena in their industries and chosen markets need to position themselves to detect threats and opportunities before they become apparent and irreversible.

Innovation and Trend Intersection

In the beginning, a trend can be an insignificant idea, hardly worth noticing. Many of these seeds die an early death, without fanfare. Chasing every idea would be silly and take too much valuable time. So, when is an idea significant enough to justify attention?

I don't know the answer; I just pay attention to the internal company environment and the external competitive landscape, and I watch and wait until something happens. I'm a big believer in remaining humble enough to maintain an open-minded perspective. For me, that is step one. This is difficult for most of us, as we are blinded by our past assumptions, education, and biases. Therefore, so many of the great trendsetters were younger than thirty years old when they began to shake the world.

Many of America's founding fathers were in their twenties. Alexander the Great conquered much of the known world before he was thirty-four. And Napoleon became first consul of the French Republic at age thirty. Many of our greatest discoveries in science also were made by people in their twenties. See a trend here?

Why don't we see wise old folks inventing new concepts? Well, I submit it isn't due to a lack of intelligence. The barrier seems clear to me: it's experience that often kills ideas and stuffs trends before they get a chance to start. As a leader, regardless of your age, you must be ready to be confused, perplexed, and mystified if you want to tune your RADAR for trend identification.

One way to key into the undercurrent of ideas is to speak with younger people in your industry. Ask open-ended questions and choke off the urge to respond to their insights, however vapid, and listen to what they have to say. Young minds are grasping for truth and understanding. They are not relying on experience, as they don't possess this yet; they just don't know how to put their thoughts and ideas into practice.

That's where you come in. Experience in application is very useful. The merger of innovative ideas and constructive experience works wonders.

It's helpful to think of the process of innovation when considering where trends dwell. Unlike invention, innovation combines existing concepts, materials, and products to create a new thing. Like mixing chocolate and peanut butter to create a peanut butter cup. Trends work that way, too.

Often, a more stable and growing trend excites people to

piggyback that direction with modifications or parallel trends that enhance or complement the first large trend. In this case, if you missed the early stages of a trend that's on fire, it doesn't mean you've missed the entire opportunity. Cell phones begat cell phone cases, and those cases became bedazzled over time with a wide range of applications.

In a way, many innovations are simply a crowdsourced response to the first macro trend. An adaptation that made perfect sense to the innovator seeking to improve his or her experience.

I've found it's valuable to set your search parameters on both early and evolving micro trends as well as on the more established macro trends that offer an opportunity for insights and maybe a business decision. I read trade articles and study thought leaders to learn how smart businesspeople seized on these trends and how they created value by doing so.

I don't look to these folks for new ideas; instead, I seek out the user population. The people doing the deed and living the experiences at the ground level. These are the innovators and trend starters. Popular dances, T-shirts, YouTube personalities—they all start from the bottom up. They hang there until a breeze begins to blow, and then the breeze becomes a gale.

The trend may be short-lived. People are fickle and move on eventually, but the effect is there for all to see. The intersection of trends is also apparent if you look in the right places. Trust me, you do not have to be clairvoyant to see the future.

A Rolling Pebble Can Become an Avalanche

A micro trend doesn't have to exist for a long time; many are fleeting. Take a battle for example. History documents countless major battles where a victorious general cites his insight in the moment as key to success. Tens of thousands of men struggling across a wide geographic area. Dust or the effects of gunpowder obscuring the terrain and the fight itself.

Great generals calmly wait for the battle to take on a rhythm. They seek to understand this rhythm and then wait for a change. A subtle shift in positions, a push in the fighting to one side or another. Maybe the sound of battle alters slightly. Great generals spoke of feeling the way the battle was trending; and in doing so, they were able to anticipate the potential outcomes and act accordingly. They are absorbing all the information and looking for a micro trend or the intersection of many micro trends to exploit those insights.

Business is a battle of sorts, but it is difficult if not impossible today to position yourself where you can see the market struggle happening all around you. As a business leader, you can use your physical observations to be sure. But you also can back that up with data collection and analysis that paints a picture for you.

It is important to evaluate what data and analysis you are receiving now in the context of trend recognition and tracking. If the people who crafted the search pattern and the analysis methodology were conventional in their approach, then you might be getting generic information that confirms expectations but misses the point.

For example, if data samples are only drawn from classic sources and analyzed with a linear mindset, you will miss out on seeing the crazy, the wild, and the special. All outcomes will conform to a "Today and tomorrow will be much like yesterday" way of thinking.

Why is it so important to be focused on all of this, especially the micro trends and ideas bubbling under the surface of business today? It's simple: the trend you miss is often the trend that knocks you and your company out of the game. If you aren't convinced a good offense will grow your company in exciting new ways, then become a trend tracker for defensive reasons.

How Early Is Too Early?

When I managed money for high-net-worth clients, the art of seeing the future clearly eluded me most of the time. I was deluged with an incredible amount of data or white noise from my firm's analysts, outside analysts, specialists, industry pundits, my peers, and my boss. My clients also fed me a steady diet of their thoughts, fears, ideas, and get-rich-quick schemes.

It took me three years to learn how to block most of this out and rely on my own personal investment philosophy. Once I was centered, I could listen and read input all day long without feeling the push and pull of opinion and emotion. I also narrowed the field by selecting a niche in the US equity market that I felt comfortable with, refusing clients who wanted to play the market, buy the latest hot IPO, or jump from one sector to the other based on a magazine article. I gave my bond business to the institutional folks in the back office and was content.

In those days, I began to see the various sectors of the markets, and the companies in those sectors, as rising, falling, or static pistons. It helped me to envision the rotations and investment flows in this way. If the piston was static, then it had two possible futures—ascend or decline. It the piston had been rising for some time, then it felt like the trend was near its end. The same was true of sectors falling for a long period.

The market sector trends usually dragged or boosted the companies or stocks living in that sector. Once I saw this in my mind's eye, I started making better investment decisions. I came to recognize that there was risk in committing too early, especially with sectors of the market that were sitting static. It was better to wait and see the clear start of movement before selling my positions or buying new ones.

As a business leader, you can create a similar understanding of your market or even the divisions and departments within your company. Awareness requires study and continuous attention to the fringe of effort as well as the core. This isn't about judging; it's about watching, listening, and waiting. The more tuned in you are, the easier it will be to see the right moment to act.

Most, if not all, commercial businesses operate in the same market sectors I observed while at UBS. There are new ones, of course, but your job is easier than mine was. All you must do is focus on your neighborhood and your organization. Micro trends take time to energize people and groups before they are noticeable to those on the outside of the excitement; but eventually, if you pay attention, you will see them evolve before they go parabolic.

Be patient. Most micro trends are duds and fade away as quickly as they started. Don't jump to conclusions too fast. With repetition, you'll begin to get the timing down.

How Late Is Too Late?

If jumping a trend early is problematic, piling on just before the trend runs its course is equally foolhardy. To continue the investment analogy, I observed people who were risk-adverse watch until the trend was a "sure thing" before committing their investment dollars.

This seemed smart and conservative to me at first. Then I saw that, often, the upward trend sputtered out and began to reverse course, descending to a static position over a short amount of time. Investors who came in too late to catch the early growth of the sector or stocks within the sector held on for the ride. They were unwilling to sell, take a small loss, and lick their wounds.

I observed and experienced this phenomenon in other areas outside the public stock markets. In 2013, the War on Terror was twelve years old. Government contracting in support of the global engagement had created thousands of new companies, making money in every way imaginable.

I watched as in 2013, the latecomers rolled in. Large defense firms, medium and small companies, finally capitulating, eager to share in the huge flow of business generated by our government. It was, alas, too late. This is what I call the eleventh-hour rush. The last push by the people who'd stood on the sidelines for eleven years, sure the war and the business associated with it wouldn't last.

By 2015, the piston was descending, and the eleventh-hour warriors were hanging on for dear life or bailing and taking their losses. Human nature is consistent when it comes to risk and reward, regardless of the topic or opportunity. There is a point where the trend is too ripe, too frothy, too overblown. Steel yourself to this scenario or your emotions will trick you into doing something imprudent and destructive. Cheer on the winners who rode the wave and look for the next ride. There's always another trend rising into prominence.

Interpreting the Tea leaves

If psychics could provide me with an edge into the way the world looks in a year or two, I'd be all over that source of inspiration. Regretfully, I don't know any business psychics, so I must rely on my individual powers of observation. I like to visualize the trajectory of the micro and macro trends I'm exposed to in a way that reveals an incremental path to one potential future.

I play the trends over and over again, like a short film in my mind. I'm attempting to anticipate the cause and effect, based on life wisdom, observations about human nature, technical knowledge, and pure guessing. It turns out you can think through a lot of possible outcomes doing this exercise. My wife knows I do this subconsciously, turning and twisting problems, challenges, and ideas until I'm ready to play soothsayer. Like all disciplines, it takes practice and time to become proficient and comfortable with the process, but it pays off.

My track record is better than most, because I've spent considerable time trying to get better at reading the tea leaves. It's much like learning how to meditate. Everyone tells you how easy it is; but when you try it, you can't seem to settle your mind down. All the thoughts swirling around in your brain are zipping all over the place, demanding attention, usually without any logic.

It takes practice and time to become proficient at meditation. I don't meditate to consider the future; I meditate to clear my mind of the present. I'm a fan, but a novice at best. I think it is easier to learn the art of prognostication than to learn many other skills. If I can do it, so can you!

Creating a Story Arc

I've published eight novels and have read everything I can find on plotting, sub-plotting, character development, and story arcs. The last concept came easy for me. SEAL missions are developed much like a story, and in my day, they were initially segmented into three simple steps, akin to the classic Greek three-act play. For SEALs, it was get in, do the deed on target, get out. Later in my career we adopted phased planning, adding two parts to create a five-phase plan: insertion, infiltration, actions on target, exfiltration, and extraction.

Our approach to phase planning kept the key five phases but fleshed out each phase by vertically listing all the micro steps required to execute each phase. We developed this planning tool as a group, throwing out any idea that made sense and then attacking it, trying to find a weakness in the idea. If it held up, it stayed. Once we had the full draft plan, it was usually eight to ten steps per phase for a total of forty to fifty action items per mission.

The next exercise was to talk the plan through, step-by-step, while asking ourselves, "What could go wrong here?" Writing fiction is easier for me because I don't have to ask a room of commandos for approval, but it follows the same logical story arc methodology.

Many macro and micro trends appear in the moment,

attractive but without a clear future. When I do find a trend, in my businesses, the stock market, even geopolitical events, I apply the story planning method and see where it leads me. I use questions like, "Then what happened?" I do this over and over to fill in the potential next steps in the trajectory of the trend. You don't have to be right when you do this exercise, just do it to become more connected to the trend and what it promises (or doesn't) going forward.

It's easy, and if you practice, then you'll be surprised how close you get to projecting the outcomes. Don't try to lock everything down tight at first; let your imagination take the wheel. You can run mental simulations, stick to a simple three-act-play format, or endeavor to detail the multiple steps the trend will follow as it rises in prominence and then, as all trends do, falls from grace. I can do this in my head but only up to a point. I'd rather jump on a whiteboard and take it to the next level.

Storyboarding the Story Arc

A technique used in film, animation, and fiction writing often is used by special operations planners to break a complex story into digestible bite-sized pieces. Storyboarding is also applicable to visionary or strategic thinking. The storyboard is a multistep construction of scenes laid out end-to-end in a linear fashion.

In cartoons, each interaction between characters is a standalone yet sequential step in a comic. Unlike phase planning, where a list is created under each phase of the mission, storyboarding allows the creator to follow the story arc at a pace set by the characters and their activity in the story.

The process is easy to learn and looks something like this: The story is of a man who enters the kitchen, looks for food to eat, finds something, makes the meal, and eats the meal before leaving the kitchen. This is a series of familiar scenes all of us could break down into separate steps, each connected front to back, progressively moving toward a satisfying end. How do we use this creative process in visionary thinking?

Let's stick with our hungry friend for a moment. If we were watching the kitchen and he walked in, stopped, and looked around, can you anticipate and project his next actions? If his face and body language convey hunger (he rubs his belly), then your storyboard of what might happen could be accurate. Of course, he could make a beeline for the junk drawer and pull out a screwdriver. This is what it feels like when you observe trends. You see what you see, and it's up to you to develop the rest of the story.

You might be wrong most of the time, but my guess is you will surprise yourself. Accuracy in this game isn't the only measure in visionary thinking. In the 1930s, you could see Nazi Germany was gearing up for war. Projecting that behavior or trend lent itself to a prediction of war in Europe, and you would have been correct. The fact that you didn't know exactly which country would be attacked first wouldn't diminish the terrifying vision your mind projected of the larger effect.

Storyboarding for strategic thought development is not project planning. With project planning, you have the end state defined for you. Your job is to build the path to that end state. Project planning isn't a journey of discovery; it's a detailed process of execution. Storyboarding starts with an idea and takes off to the horizon, searching for the outcome.

Logic is important, but logic is biased to the past. It's acceptable to toss in a lack of logic and see where it takes you. In the World War II example, Germany was certainly getting ready for war, and everyone around them knew it was the case. So why didn't anybody stop Hitler before he started the war? Logic is the reason. Britain's navy far eclipsed that of Germany; they ruled the seas. France's air force and land army dwarfed Hitler's forces.

Nobody believed an undersized nation crawling back from

the losses of the first World War would go on the offensive against overwhelming odds. Yet that is exactly what Hitler did. Use abstractions, wild card events, and illogic to develop and test your storyboard hypothesis. The odder the trend, the more likely it will burn a bright new path into the future, instead of simply extending the past forward.

Timeline, End State, and Impact

Now for the most difficult part of trend spotting, trend tracking, and trend projection: determining the timeline, end state, and impact of the trend in question. This is the payoff, the value proposition for participating in a visionary thought experiment. Think of Adolf Hitler.

If someone in 1935 had a good idea of Hitler's timeline for war in Europe—anticipating his strategic goals and understanding the impact a technologically advanced world war would have on the global population over the following decade—then maybe someone would've tried to stop him before he started.

Business is never as dire as world conflict but being able to see the future in more finite terms has benefits. Business trends, large and small, tell. Like a gambler watching the micro facial twitches of his opponent, you too can hone a skill for spotting insignificant movements born of passion and develop a feel for when a new idea surges through your company, market, or industry like an electric shock.

I suggest you practice storyboarding, projecting multiple end states. Run these lines of thought to the horizon and contemplate the impact each projection represents. Not all trends become significant outcomes. And one person's measure of impact might not align with other evaluators, eager to score and report on the trend's status, progress, or demise. Consider the impact of the hula hoop. The concept has been around since 500 BC, but was made popular in modern times by the toy company Wham-O. Since 1958, millions of hula hoops have been produced and sold.

The total sales associated with this toy is stunning, but has it been as impactful as the introduction of the car? The telephone? The smart phone? You see my point. Determining how impactful the outcome may be is key to understanding how it will affect your company—for better or worse. A visionary leader is an asset if they are practitioners in trend tracking. Be valuable.

Chapter Eight

Threat Recognition

Not everything that is faced can be changed, but nothing can be changed until it is faced.
James Baldwin

To a pessimist, all the world's a threat. "Risk mitigation" is a catchy business management phrase that gets tossed around by leaders and managers who know that it, in conjunction with management, can slow the rocket down. It slows it down to a speed that is comfortable. Not loud or scary, not unpredictable. Steady, safe, and warm.

Of course, the purpose of a rocket isn't to behave like this at all. Its purpose is to survive a violent and controlled explosion, to soar and seek out the objective programmed into its navigation system. Whether it's a flight to the moon, to place a satellite in earth's orbit, or to hit an enemy target, rockets cannot "sort of" get there. They need to be set free and be allowed to challenge the laws of physics on the way to their designed destiny.

A racehorse that's not allowed to run fast, a champion chess master forced to play at a child's pace...these things sound silly. But replace these examples with small business and fast-growing enterprise, and you will begin to see the point. A business is a vehicle, a platform, designed to achieve financial gain. It isn't created to mope along or barely pay the bills. Its purpose is to grow, to soar, to challenge the laws of business physics.

The law of competition, the law of scaling, the law of positioning...I know you're following me now. So, why is it trendy, "smart," and intellectual to strap shackles on a business in the spirit of risk mitigation? If you can't have reward without risk, then eliminating risks also reduces or removes the probability of reward.

Why We Are Fearful

It's amazing our species has survived this long. Hundreds of thousands of years ago, we humans were on the run or hiding from everything else on the planet that was trying to eat us for dinner. We didn't have fangs or claws, and our young offspring were completely unable to fend for themselves until they were four or five years old.

We developed deep instincts for survival and learned to use the only advantage we had over the rest of the fauna: our brain. The amygdala is the oldest part of the human brain, and it still alerts us to danger. Our ancient instinct to live is intact. This aversion to risk is hardwired in us all. We are born and learn how to fear in a new way, through our parents.

As a father of five and grandfather of five, I have some experience being a parent and observing parenting firsthand. While we aren't being chased by sabertoothed tigers and giant sloths anymore, the early stages of human growth are still fraught with risk. We are taught to be fearful of, or at a minimum concerned about, heat, cold, being dirty, high things, dark places, diseases, sharp things, fast things, and strangers.

By the time we are ten years old, we have a new set of operating instructions overlayed onto our primal software. This process works as intended. We rarely hear of a child dying from a terrible stove burn or from juggling steak knives. Parents do the right thing and teach their children to survive, and most do survive.

Of course, most children grow to be adults who continue for the rest of their lives to see risks everywhere, heeding both their primal intuition and their parent's warnings regarding anything strange, different, or too exciting. I was raised in this same manner. To say this mindset is limiting is an understatement.

Navy SEALs appear, from the outside looking in, to be fearless warriors, who not only laugh at risk but seek risk. The movies portray us as wild and crazy, living on the edge without a care in the world as we execute high missions in the name of freedom and, yes, fun. Some of this stereotype of the elite American warrior breed might be true. Risktakers usually have a well-developed sense of humor. So, a casual observer, doing research for a film or television show, might get the wrong impression.

Humor is how risktakers cope with their internal alarms going off. They are human like the rest of us, driven by those same primal and parental inputs. We all must fear failure, fear injury. Humor is a positive emotion, and when shared between warriors just before a night parachute jump or a combat insertion, it is an effective counter to the dark thoughts.

I was eighteen years old when I joined the SEALs. At that point in life, my greatest challenge had been trying to surf the big waves in Hawaii. I was born in Nebraska, so any wave was a big wave to me. When I started to learn how to surf, there was a constant distraction interfering with my learning curve. I was convinced that the ocean was trying to kill me, one wave at a time.

Eventually I learned how to handle the waves rolling into Waikiki beach, three- to five-feet high, and they became less and less challenging. So, I decided to go to the north shore and up my game. That was a mistake. The waves were significantly bigger, more powerful. At many beaches, they broke over coral. Getting sliced and diced was a new part of surfing for me.

I did my best, but never became good enough in my two years living in Hawaii to become comfortable surfing the north side of Oahu. This did, however, prepare me to face the waves crashing off the southern coast of Coronado, California, the home of basic SEAL training.

My six months as a basic SEAL trainee taught me things about human nature and coping with fear that you just can't learn by reading books or watching movies. We all are products of our early influences and primal wiring. Cautious, worried, and determined to avoid failure and injury by not taking any risks.

Of course, SEAL training is about forcing you to face your fears. The ones who voluntarily quit, often did so long before they arrived at the threshold of true risk. It was their perception of risk that drove them to avoid the "inevitable" by leaving the program.

Later, when I returned as a leader in the SEAL basic school, I was able to observe this self-selection process firsthand and objectively. I realized that the evolution of a person from student to potential Navy SEAL was all about how each coped with and managed risk.

Repetition of risk-taking reduces fear of risk-taking. The SEAL selection process is all about repetition. Challenge after challenge, a mix of tests is presented that provide the students with lots of opportunities to grow and win or whither and quit. All these years later, I'm convinced risk-taking is a learned skill, and we can all become better through repetition and frequent exposure to challenges that push our limits and make us more and more comfortable with risk-taking.

So, why am I spending time in a book about vision and strategy telling you about how Navy SEALs and other elite professionals handle risk? Two reasons. First, to take bold audacious action is a great risk. Those who dare to do so will face fear of failure on a regular basis and have their level of commitment chipped away by the many who fear the risk of trying more than winning. The second reason is so you can correlate the connection between fear, risk, and threats.

What Is a Threat?

Put simply, a threat is whatever triggers a fear response in any of us. Most threats are constructs of our mind, struggling to understand new information that hasn't been accepted, analyzed, and scored for risk. I like to think of threats much the same way we did in the SEALs. There were long-range threats, mid-range threats, short-range threats, and close-range threats. We had detection methods and weapons aligned with each type of threat.

The trick was to detect the threat with enough time to address it with the appropriate counterresponse. Air strikes for far threats; mortars and sniper rifles for mid-range threats; rifles, machineguns, and grenades for short-range threats; and knives, fists, and knees for close-range threats. The point is: if you can see all potential threats with enough time to fight or flee, then you can survive most situations.

The gravity of the threat often is dependent on your organization's capability to defend, divert, or defeat the threat. Given enough time, one of these actions should work. In business we are usually talking about longer durations from threat detection to impact than in a combat environment.

Considering what I've discussed with you in the previous paragraphs, you should instinctively realize that a person's perception of threats and their perception of adverse consequences associated with a threat are elevated, neutral, or diminished, depending on their risk tolerance.

To a person with a low risk tolerance, threats are everywhere, and they are all catastrophic. As a visionary leader, you will have to assess your risk aversion and philosophy on consequence analysis. You also will need to understand that those around you—your bosses, your team—may have different views of what constitutes a threat.

Assuming you are neutral or comfortable looking at threats, your job will be to communicate to others what is happening, when it may happen, what impact to expect, and most importantly, how you and your team are going to deal with the threat. Never assume others around you are gamblers. Most people are not, and they need leadership to guide them through their initial fear response to a constructive battle plan.

In 2015, my business partner and I sold a defense company to the employees, creating what is known as an ESOP. I stayed on as CEO. After the hard work of closing the deal was complete, I looked to the future, seeking threats to the new structure. When you sell your company to the employees, a bank or private equity firm underwrites the deal, handing checks to the sellers.

The day before we closed, we had zero debt and two million plus dollars in the bank. The day after the sale, the new employee-owned entity had zero cash in the bank and was one hundred percent in debt. Our loans to the lender who made the deal possible would now be paid off by the ESOP over the next seven to ten years.

Planning for a Long-Range Threat

ESOPs are great. But as the newly minted CEO of an ESOP, the gravity of being in so much debt was hard to fathom. While I didn't see any threats on the horizon, the feeling I had was less than optimistic. I'd personally never been in great debt, and now I was responsible for a company that had to grow its way out of the situation. We also had to pay the monthly interest on the ESOP debt, which was a drain on working capital.

Because it was essentially a new business model, I began to look at our business differently. I started to ask good questions, following the "what if" approach to eliciting answers. This involved many people and took a month or so. My chief financial officer was a great help during this analysis.

At UBS, I'd learned over time how to evaluate companies and how to anticipate the winds of market fortune and the effects of those trends on individual businesses. Was there a tailwind accelerating growth and good results? Or was there a headwind slowing the company down, making it difficult to grow or even survive?

I simplified this analysis by thinking through three scenarios. I labeled them A, B, and C. The A scenario was a track showing a greater than twenty percent angle of ascent in business growth. An ascent that might rely on a tailwind positively affecting the industry or a new product breakthrough. The B scenario was the flat trajectory outlook. Nothing great, but nothing scary either. The third probability trend was the C scenario. It was the mirror opposite of the A scenario. Trending and descending, twenty percent or more.

We determined that the long-range threat to our defense company was a drawdown of forces in the Middle East as the War on Terror ended. We primarily trained soldiers, Marines, coastguards, and federal law enforcement in counter- and anti-terrorism tactics and skills.

While there wasn't a declared drawdown in sight, we decided to use that as the headwind and game out the consequences. We applied the A, B, C evaluation and trend calculation. We also loaded consequences to each trendline. Scenario A was favorable, so there was no need to mitigate. Scenario B wasn't too bad either, so we focused on scenario C. It was this hypothetical that forced me to conclude we needed another way to make money, and we had twenty-four to thirty-six months to make it happen.

At first, the idea was to acquire another small defense company that had the promise of great margins for the next four to six years. This was a company not related to the War on Terror. I took a few months off as CEO to focus on this search, while my able chief operating officer ran the business. What I found was disappointing.

The best defense sector I could find was cybersecurity. I met with many cyber experts and several CEOs of cyber companies. What I heard wasn't making me feel better. That sector was sexy and all the rage on television and in the news, but cyber as a sector of the market was fractured and multitiered. Cyber and IT experts were starting to be plentiful in the marketplace, commoditizing staffing as a way to play with juicy margins.

Much of the technology was fleeting. Shelf lives for new ideas were getting shorter and shorter. Invent or die was the motto of the day. I decided it was time to look elsewhere; it was time to ask the board to allow us to buy a commercial company.

In the end, it was a great strategic move. We bought a small commercial healthcare company in late 2016, and it grew exponentially for the next five years. As anticipated, the department of defense and the federal government began to defund counter- and anti-terror programs, beginning in 2017.

Our strategy to offset the burden of ESOP debt servicing worked like a charm. Did I know it would turn out this way in the spring of 2015? Of course not. Lots of things could have gone wrong. My board of directors put my idea through the wringer, and I needed to prove, as much as I was able, that the strategy was viable.

In the end, I received the approval I required to execute. Of course, my instinct for long-range scanning and planning could have been a recipe for disaster if I were wrong. Being visionary isn't about being perfect or exactly right. It's about slowly turning the "battleship" to a new course over time. It takes help from everyone to make a visionary strategy successful.

I've spent much of this chapter and the first part of this book explaining how hard it is to believe in yourself when all around you doubt and throw stones. The plan to buy a healthcare company was a tough sell. I ran a company that focused on tactics and terrorism. But in the end, all were persuaded to give it a shot. The rest, as they say, is history.

Contingency Planning and Threat Interdiction

The fancy military jargon for an ambush is interdiction. Technically, it means to intercept, to interrupt. But there you go. It's jargon. If you were a tribal chieftain three thousand years ago in Europe and were told by the scouts posted on the edge of your territory that a raiding band of warriors was heading toward you and your people, you as the leader would have decisions to make. If this was a rather frequent occurrence or there was memory of a devastating raid in the tribe's past, then you might already have plans in place to deal with it happening again.

These plans are contingency plans. Another product of "what if" thinking. Having contingency plans reduces the need for panicked communications and last-minute reactions to an impending threat. They don't cost anything to have ready. And once in place, they can mean the difference between success and failure when the threat arrives at your door.

Visionary leadership isn't always about seizing opportunity. Often, it's about anticipating and preparing for a threat. Threats tend to be easier for a leader and others to identify, while opportunity isn't a topic our parents or our teachers taught us to recognize. I'll say it again: we are fear-focused and tuned in to see threats everywhere.

A world half empty is the expectation of many. And even if you gain ground, something or someone is bound to ruin it for us. I have a hard time with this because I've learned to be optimistic. To expect the best, not the worst. To believe any threat can be dealt with and eliminated or bypassed. Contingency planning is the first step.

In our tribal scenario, the leader has a day, tops, to prepare his village for an attack. A solid contingency plan for this situation might involve piles of arrows and spears waiting for use, trenches, pits, and moats, built long before and maintained to protect the perimeter. Piles of brush bundled and ready to be tossed into the trench and set ablaze as another barrier.

The men may have staged more weapons and supplies outside the village, near the route an attacking group would follow. Traps may be in position along trails that the young boys will place in position and set. Food and water supplies will be staged also. Maybe a local cave will serve as a redoubt, a place of safety for the old, the young, and the infirm, protected by a small team of warriors.

All this can be accomplished far in advance of a threat arriving down the valley. If the entire village is prepared, trained, and ready to do their part, then victory is possible and maybe even probable.

If you are a leader and your organization doesn't have contingency plans in place, then my question is, "Why not?" Threats to businesses come in all shapes and sizes. Mitigating those threats with insurance products, cash reserves, pre-purchased commodities and supplies, and contingency training for all your people are just a few things you can do to prepare. The other thing you can do is think the big thoughts.

Look to the horizon and sweep three hundred and sixty degrees to detect looming threats. Being prepared in general is a must, and I strongly suggest you do this as soon as it is practical. Waiting for the threat to appear, even if you're prepared for the worst, isn't much of a strategy.

That's where threat interdiction comes in. You need to plot an intercept course, evaluate the level of threat and consequences the threat represents, and determine the threat timeline, as much as you can. In my example, we were a newly minted ESOP company with no clear indication a threat to our business and to our margins was anywhere in the future.

We used logic to play out the timeline and determine the consequences. In our case, we were correct in our assumptions and had intercepted the threat timeline by initiating a counterstrategy almost three years in the making. I worked for another large defense firm that believed the boom in government contracting services to the commercial sector would never end. When it did, they were caught flatfooted and struck dumb by the implications.

A few years of careful domestic business development and selective acquisitions would have smoothed out what turned out to be a very rough road for several years. Preparing for, searching for, and dealing with future threats is what visionary leaders do. Be visionary!

Chapter Nine

Seeing Opportunities

Expect change. Analyze the landscape. Take the opportunities. Stop being the chess piece; become the player. It's your move.
Tony Robbins

Spotting opportunities is a gift, an art, a knack. At least it seems that way to me. Studies show that people are motivated more by avoiding loss than by pursuing gain. It goes right back to the part of our brain that's hardwired to detect and avoid risk. We do have biology that rewards us when we find pleasure in having a positive self-esteem, social affection, a great physical workout, and love.

You must put yourself out there in some manner to reap the rewards of the serotonin, dopamine, oxytocin, and endorphins surging through your system. I wish there were a fifth chemical that made us feel great when we spotted a great opportunity, but, alas, this isn't the case.

I frequently use quotes when writing or when contemplating the wisdom of others, regardless of the subject or era of the author. Many thoughts and observations are timeless. Yes, perhaps it's bumper sticker philosophy, but for me it works. As I scan the Internet, there are an overwhelming number of quotes and inspirational thoughts related to the subject of opportunity.

In my opinion, there are two types of opportunity. The first type comes knocking on your door. It's easily recognized, sitting right in front of you, daring you to do something. The second type is less visible, more difficult to detect.

When Opportunity Knocks

Decision-making is key to seizing the day. I spent a lot of time in part one of this book dwelling on the attributes, disciplines, and decision-making skills required to be a successful visionary leader. The vast multitudes of managers, executives, and business owners either don't have the knowledge and skill to make the call; or if they do, they lack the courage, conviction, and vision required to take hold of the opportunities that tumble into their laps.

You have a choice. There is no way I can eliminate the fears and concerns associated with a glass-half-full view of the world. Only you can change that dynamic. Or, if you are ready to execute, only you can sustain that winning mindset.

In the special operations world, we focus on precision, but prepare for the sloppy and unpredictable reality of warfare. We spend huge amounts of money to gain certainty, but rarely find confirmation of our assumptions when we get to the target. On one operation overseas, I took my SEAL platoon on multiple search missions looking for weapons stockpiles. We planned, prepared, studied, and then flew in at night or at dawn to raid neighborhoods where intelligence sources told us the bad guys hid their weapons.

Another time, after failing yet again to find any weapons in people's homes, I took my platoon out of the congested cluster of shanty homes on a ridgeline and down to a large open soccer field adjacent to a school. My communications guy called in the checklist code phrase for failure and requested helicopter extraction. As we waited on a perimeter, people began to flood the soccer field. Families for the most part and lots of kids, laughing and running all over the place.

As I kneeled there, contemplating all the effort wasted on another dry hole, one of my men—a highly talented individual who spoke five languages and who would later be decorated for his heroism during the Black Hawk Down incident in Somalia—approached me with a proposition. The kids, he said, were babbling about weapons and bullets in the school. He pointed to the one-story brick complex behind me as he spoke. He suggested we investigate. I didn't have authorization to search a school; and now with hundreds of civilians surrounding our perimeter, my first instinct was to shoot down his idea. Then I changed my mind. I directed him to speak with a few adults to confirm the rumor and report back to me.

An hour later the army was still busy transferring the cases of guns, grenades, and bullets from the school to their waiting helicopters. The kids were right. In the bright light of such a terrific find, nobody questioned my decision to take down the school without the authority to do so. It was all about the win.

Opportunity Is All Around Us

It's a sad truth that when disaster strikes, opportunity abounds. It's the circle of life to some extent. One person's lost job is another's new job offer. A natural calamity spawns reconstruction work for hundreds of small companies. This occurs all around us every day. Serial entrepreneurs live for adverse economic situations. They swoop down and buy distressed property or oversold stock; they seize opportunity in the vacuum created by people and companies too stunned and cowed by the negative event to take positive action.

This goes back to my thoughts on risk perception from the last chapter. Emotional swings in the stock market, unrelated to the actual value of the underlying companies the stock represents, allows smart value investors to buy quality at a discount. The same thing happens in the real estate market, just with longer swing periods.

When I was a kid, opportunity came in two forms: freedom from school and chores or a way to make a few dollars. A Coke bottle sitting in the grass on a vacant lot was a few blocks away from money in my pocket (we collected glass bottles to return to local stores for change). An overgrown front yard belonging to an elderly couple represented a potential mowing gig, and so on. As mentioned earlier, we were not taught to seek opportunity per se, but we were taught that America was the land of opportunity.

Our history studies included stories about settlers coming from other countries to start a new life. Suffering cold and starvation to scratch out a little world all their own. To me, this seemed the recipe for advancement when you didn't grow up rich. So, I kept my eyes open for opportunity.

Another interesting truth is the way opportunity is almost manufactured by people blind to the possibilities pulsing all around them. These folks decline to invest in anything that isn't a slam-dunk certainty, leaving room for others to step in, regardless of the type of investment. They leave jobs because they aren't "fulfilled," rather than staying longer, leveraging their position to build up a nest egg, and allowing them time to create an audacious plan of action.

A new business, a special school to achieve a key certification, or just to travel and take a break. Every situation, in and outside of employment, is a learning situation, an opportunity to become smarter, sharper, tougher. This form of opportunity is also valuable, yet rarely seized upon.

The Opportunity Mindset

Here's the million, or maybe billion-dollar question. I described a few examples in the prior paragraphs, and I could go on and on, filling pages with examples and scenarios. But I won't. It's the old "teach a person to fish" rule. It's far better for you to understand the mindset that enables you to remove your blindfold than to have opportunities specifically listed for you.

In my first business book, *Be Nimble,* I spent considerable time emphasizing the need to have humility, to be humble. This is a key to the opportunity mindset as well. If the formula stated earlier (risk equals opportunity) is true, then being humble and open-minded helps you see the opportunities with a clear mind.

The challenge for most people embracing the mindset is they go too far. Everything is now a valuable opportunity, and no risk is worth evaluating. They shift from an all fear and hesitation leader into a crazy, brave, shiny object chaser. As in most things, prudence and moderation have a part to play here.

Being open-minded to what opportunities may lay in the ashes isn't the same as highly energized thrill seeking. Instead, it is a state of humble absorption. Soaking up the real and now, without the past interfering with your perception of the potential opportunity. Prior education, awards, failures, traditions, processes, etc., must be pushed aside to allow for this pure observation and evaluation. That's why I refer to this as an opportunity mindset.

If you can look beyond your hard-wired brain and your lifetime of risk mitigation indoctrination, then you have come halfway to being a successful opportunity hunter. The second half is establishing the humble mindset. Practice to make this new approach a habit. Make the habit a method you apply repeatedly, until it becomes second nature to step up, see the opportunity, clear the baggage from your mind, and evaluate.

Extraordinarily successful investors have years of experience practicing this system. Regardless of the investment type, practice shortens the feedback loop in the brain, and soon these professionals are finding and processing opportunities as easily as breathing.

In 2015, I took a short hiatus as CEO to focus on a diversification strategy enabled by a planned acquisition. My COO ran day-to-day operations, allowing me time to study the competitive terrain and the trends in markets I understood. Then I began looking at markets and opportunities I distinctly did not understand. I soon picked up trends and movements that indicated things were about to change in a big way in the healthcare space.

However, what I saw wasn't what the market experts were

excited about. They were shouting loud and clear that technology was going to disrupt healthcare and that, combined with the Affordable Care Act (Obamacare), the healthcare industry was about to make a titanic move. A move predicted to displace the status quo and rattle everyone's lethargic cages.

The words disruption and healthcare were always aligned with technology and the ACA in industry books and periodicals. This made it much easier for my company to buy a truly disruptive care delivery model and scale it for three years before the pundits and the market thinkers saw what we were doing. I believe it was my initial opportunity mindset, and the intelligent and enthusiastic people who built the dream into a reality, that turned an idea into a market mover.

Detection and Evaluation

Detecting an opportunity isn't always a conscious, deliberate act. Serendipity plays a part, too. Going on a run in a different part of the neighborhood and bumping into an old acquaintance who's relocating and must unload his home at a severe discount, for example. I scan for opportunity every day.

Maintaining the opportunity mindset, I believe, opens the universe in a way that allows serendipity to find you. I stay alert in general, listen to strangers and strange things. I'd read and watch oblique sources; in other words, stay humble, open, and pay attention. By doing this, you will find more than enough opportunity to evaluate. Applying this process to your leadership role in a business channels and reduces the volume of insights, but they are still there for you to recognize and evaluate.

Evaluating an opportunity can follow several paths. The first path is a quick assessment. Gut feeling, experience applied, feels exciting; and it bears further thought or action. When I get these feelings, I write down the quick assessment. Often, I use my cell phone as my way of documenting the inspiration and initial thoughts. I text or email a short paragraph to myself for later contemplation.

The next path is a bit more energetic and involved. I may see an opportunity and have an epiphany that compels me to drop what I'm doing, find a safe place to think, and start scribbling my epiphany onto or into any device or platform that I have access to. In this mode, I might spend an hour or two fleshing out a written evaluation of what the opportunity represents. Upside, downside, any aspect of the opportunity that defines a potential commitment to a path forward. I get ideas for novels and follow this more dramatic pattern, fearing I'll forget or lose the essence of the epiphany if I delay concentrated thought and evaluation of the idea.

The third path to evaluating an opportunity can occur as a sequential function of the first two methods. An evolutionary building of raw ideas to an inspired skeleton of a plan, and finally a full evaluation and analysis as a prelude to deploying resources to seize the promise the opportunity seems to present.

This third method is often the way we as leaders are introduced to an idea. Somebody else has an epiphany, an idea, an insight; and they galvanize the organization to assess, evaluate, risk score, and create a plan to execute. If you are the source, the person initiating this deeper dive, you now have a communications task in front of you.

Your epiphany is exciting...to you. Now you must fire up the troops. Describe the opportunity in optimistic terms. "We are going to put a man on the moon. You people in this room are going to make that happen! I know there are a million challenges to address and conquer, but we will push forward, one challenge at a time, until will persevere!" Once you've dragged others into your madness, help them do their job evaluating the opportunity with verve and alacrity! Visionaries lead the way!

Distraction or Strategic Moment?

Besides finding, identifying, and evaluating opportunities, a visionary leader must monetize the idea and take it to its natural horizon. Will the initiative be a game changer? Will it significantly change the financials? Will it block a rising competitor? And if it does any or all of these things, then what is the return on investment? Spending three million to save or make a few million isn't smart.

In my personal experience, and from countless discussions with other leaders over the years, it is this final hurdle that stops most ideas from becoming the next big thing. As a leader, you must understand that the return on investment (ROI) is critical to receiving the green light in most if not all business organizations. I suggest you bring in an expert in calculating the upfront costs, the sustained costs, and the financial payoff. You'll need a timeline showing the start-up, ramp-up, ongoing operations, and the point in time where the business idea breaks even and becomes profitable. Never gain an audience with a senior decision maker to pitch your visionary plan without checking this important box first.

Another barrier to success is your track record. If you routinely think in strategic terms and randomly fire ideas at your senior leaders without a real analysis and plan in hand, then you'll lose credibility and have a harder time getting the audience you need when you are ready to present in a serious way. The label I hear frequently is shiny object. A person becomes known for chasing things that sound cool and inspiring, but never see the interior of a boardroom for approval.

If you have suffered this plight, then I'm right there with you. I write about these missteps because I've been that guy. Discounted, ignored, and rarely taken seriously. It wasn't until I received some astute mentoring that I was able to structure and prepare my pitch appropriately. Once I did that, my approval rate rose dramatically. Even if your idea isn't approved, you will gain the respect of the decision makers for doing it right.

If you are the top decision maker, think about what I've just shared. Are there bright people in your business or organization who carry the stigma of chasing shiny objects? In a search for meaningful inspiration, ingenuity, and visionary thought leadership within your span of leadership control, why not create a training and mentoring program to teach would-be Einsteins and Edisons how to find, evaluate, develop, monetize, and pitch new ideas?

Go and No-Go

In the military and in the SEAL teams, making a key decision is often referred to as pulling the trigger. It implies finality and total commitment to the task at hand. Making the decision to pursue an idea through the various phases of development up to and through the approval process involves several decision points. In the SEALs, we refer to these key milestones or gates as go and no-go points.

Leading visionary change requires you to make many small and large decisions. Decisions made without the full knowledge of the future and rarely a full understanding of the challenges. Managers make decisions every day, but the scope and scale of their decisions are limited to the processes, systems, procedures, and policies in place. It is, in fact, their job to follow well-thought-out guidelines. There is little that is unknown and there is little risk involved in making these decisions. Chasing and deciding to seize an opportunity is different.

On a special operations mission, the entire storyline is segmented into small bits or phases. The leaders are allowed great autonomy to make the call in the moment, based on the facts at hand. However, there are controls imposed on these leaders by senior mission commanders, which allow for a pause of sorts. A pause at key points in the mission's progress to determine if all is still aligned with success.

This continuous series of go-no-go opportunities allows the entire leadership structure a way to reevaluate the big plan and confirm their assumptions. If the assumptions change, the leaders evaluate if the plan has lost its luster and its probability of succeeding. I suggest doing the same thing for a new initiative.

I've followed this approach for several years now as I pursue new opportunities from first thought to execution. I've succeeded more than I've failed; and when I failed, it was usually due to having too much enthusiasm. Enthusiasm is great and it makes work fun, but I found, at least with me, it blinds me. So I don't see, or I disregard reality over time as the original assumptions shift and change.

In the run-up to the famous battle of Waterloo, Napoleon Bonaparte conceived a brilliant plan to attack the Prussians first, before they could join and reinforce with the British under the Duke of Wellington. This scheme initially succeeded. The Prussians were smashed and left the field in France's hands. Napoleon assumed that the Prussian army was in full retreat. He directed one of his marshals to follow the Prussians closely to prevent them from regrouping and circling back.

This assumption, and the failure of the marshal to closely observe the Prussians as ordered, set in motion Napoleon's defeat. Later in the day, while fully engaged in a battle fighting the British, Napoleon was told the Prussians had in fact looped around and were going to arrive soon to reinforce the British. Napoleon ignored this new information; and rather than pull out of the battle and live to fight another day, he doubled down on beating Wellington.

In the end, the Battle of Waterloo was lost by one of the world's greatest military minds because he refused to accept that his brilliant plan was rendered invalid by reality on the ground. Waterloo has evolved over time into a literal synonym for disaster. Once you've decided to roll the dice, you should establish milestones, checks and balances, and go-no-go points to prevent your ego or your enthusiasm from overriding reality.

Vision Vs Optimization

When I first entered the commercial business world, the adversary was tradition. Tradition trumped thought. Tradition was the primary reason companies failed to innovate; and the leaders of most companies were the keepers of the sacred flame, not the lead disrupters and change agents. That has changed over time. Tradition wasn't defeated by smart employees challenging the status quo; it was changed by competition from overseas and by the rapid intrusion of technology.

Technology turned everything on its head, and the rise of competent global competitors forced our economy to streamline, to optimize. Now, in my opinion, the rise of optimization as an end state, as a replacement for strategy and audacious leadership, is the adversary. I doubt Rembrandt prepared to paint a masterpiece by first measuring and limiting the amount of paint to be used on his project.

I will address optimization more frequently and in greater detail further along in this book. It is a valuable management method when applied logically and appropriately. However, I feel that most highly optimized companies are dead in the water. Polishing and sharpening to their heart's delight, while the universe changes all around them. And they, oblivious to the macro implications of these changes, happily swap vision for leanness.

The vision thing, at the end of the day, is much more difficult to grasp and pursue. It is not concrete. It is not easily measured. As a Lean Six Sigma Master Black Belt, I understand the proper use of systems and process analysis, diagnosis, and the spirit of continuous improvement. But some things in nature and in business are not improved by linear reasoning and incremental adaptations. Some things, like butterflies, start as one thing and transform, naturally, into something completely different.

You are a leader. You should not be cowed by the philosophy of business optimization. Instead, you should understand and embrace optimization as a method to clean things up after you've shaken things up. Seeking and then pursuing opportunity is deliberately destructive and a threat to the status quo and those represented by the status quo. The enemy of optimization is chaos and change, especially visionary change.

Visionary change is the purposeful incitement of chaos, at least in the short run. You will be confronted by the new tradition. Stability, security, and comfort are delivered not by dynamic leadership and vision, but by optimization. Your people will be fearful of your initiatives because they threaten their professional sense of meaning and purpose. They are invested in the now and are recognized for their contributions based on the current paradigm. This is normal, and you must prepare for this inevitability.

You will never convince everybody your opportunity is worth the self-inflicted chaos; but trust me, it is the only way to ensure the long-term survival of your business. Be bold, look for opportunity everywhere, and be strong enough to seize those opportunities that make strategic sense. It's called leadership.

Chapter Ten

Building Your Dream Team

A genuine leader is not a searcher for consensus but a molder of consensus.

Dr. Martin Luther King, Jr.

I spent the formative part of my life in an organization fondly referred to by its members as "the teams." A Navy SEAL operates in small elements and does so in the most hostile of environments. When things go wrong for a group of SEALs, they must rely on each other to execute and survive. They know this and are proud to be a part of an elite unit that is more effective and efficient because of its ability to bond and leverage teamwork.

SEALs are selected for attributes that lend themselves to bonding, to gelling as a team, a family. They also are screened for their ability to commit to a noble purpose intellectually, a purpose that may be the cause of their demise. This isn't media or entertainment hype; it's real. I've never experienced anything like it outside of the SEAL teams.

It took me years to realize that SEAL-level team building is outside the realm of possibility for most companies, and it makes sense that that's the case. Military elites are the pointy end of the spear, the cutting edge of national policy. Many times, using a special operations unit is all that's required to do the job. I concluded that I was blessed by being a part of that experience, a brotherhood of special people dedicated—and that's an important distinction—to being the best they can be as individuals and, more importantly, as a team.

Civilians are not screened, selected, or trained in the same manner as Navy SEALs. And a job is rarely considered a noble calling for most employees. There are exceptions, of course. People focused on saving lives: police, firefighters, medical professionals, and many people associated with helping the poor. These folks are altruistic and committed to a purpose greater than themselves. But most other professions do not demand this level of selflessness and sacrifice. What to do?

A visionary leader without a team to pursue and achieve a vison is nothing more than a philosopher. To execute, you require your own SEAL team. An elite crew of your own choosing, a group of technically and spiritually aligned professionals that can suffer through failure and not give up. You need a dream team to reach your dream.

Early Stage—Envisioning a New Future

It's difficult to envision a different and more exciting future surrounded by people who see the world through eyes dimmed by the fear of risk-taking. When asked by people what a new SEAL student should do to improve the odds of graduating our basic training and selection course, I give them this simple answer: Associate with happy people. Stay away from the sad sacks.

If repeating affirmations effectively influences motivation and confidence, hanging with happy and enthusiastic people is one hundred times as effective. If a SEAL student aligns with one or more fellow students who are contemplating the worst-case scenario as soon as the sun rises each day, that student is doomed to fail.

The opposite is also true. Happy people, and happy SEAL students, use humor to offset negative feelings. They poke fun, sing, dance, and belittle the pain and suffering. They do this not because they are stupid or oblivious to reality, but because they understand, deep inside, that a positive outlook is a recipe for survival and success.

The same holds true in business. If your current leadership

structure is riddled with naysayers and grumpy risk mitigators, you will be dragged down, or at least influenced. Imagine conceiving a wonderful thought about the future and handing it to these folks to chase. The result is a forgone conclusion. They will kill it. Any idea that challenges the status quo (think comfort zone) is a threat to be...here it comes...mitigated. In the early stages of idea generation and conceptual thinking, you need to be open to the possibilities.

At this point in the game, your team also must be open-minded and willing to dream, to dare, to question the way things are, and to contemplate a world where everything can be different. These people may have to be assembled artificially; my guess is for most of you this will be the case.

It would be unlikely to find five or six Steve Jobses in one department, division, or senior leadership team. I suggest you keep your eye out for these special minds. Remember them. Create a team of dreamers on paper for the day when you need them. This won't be popular with your subordinate leaders or people with titles that declare they are the only ones empowered to oversee planning or long-range thinking.

If the title includes the word strategy, you have a fifty-fifty chance of getting lucky, of finding someone who is the real deal and could perhaps lead your dream team. But if they can't, then you must save the team. You must not assemble this cluster of optimistic minds and then place them under a leader who falls into the naysayer class.

I suggest you facilitate the team's engagement with an idea by tossing it to them with a list of questions. Don't feed them your conclusions or your early analysis (at this point, it's probably positive and you're already leaning forward). Don't give them too much time to brainstorm. The more time they have, the more their project planning and risk management education and experience will kick-in.

Given enough time, even the most open-minded people tend

to default to structure and normalcy. Initially, I'd give them three hours to answer your questions and come up with more of their own. Let them brief you on the work product. Record or somehow capture the insights and strive to listen and absorb instead of direct and challenge their assumptions and thoughts.

This will be hard for most effective leaders, but it is valuable to let their enthusiasm run free. If they perceive you have a direction in mind, then they will moderate their views and begin to conform to what they think the boss wants.

Evaluating the Threat or Opportunity

The open mindset required to dream big, think big, and consider crazy is different from the mindset required to evaluate the distinct pros and cons of a visionary concept. There are detail-oriented dreamers with legitimate project management skills; and if you have employees like this, then consider yourself blessed.

More often, the two types of people are separated by their passions. Dreamers will dream and managers will manage. This means you may have to create a second team to perform the evaluation process. As noted in the last two chapters, threats and opportunities live side-by-side on the horizon. Your business can benefit from early detection and consideration of these potential game changers by engaging them as early as possible.

Evaluating threats means gaming the positives and negatives associated with a new competitor, a new economic environment, a new law, or new products and services that will challenge or severely impact your organization's future success. By now you understand that threats also can be opportunities for you to exploit. A trend that might harm you three years in the future can reveal a way to pivot your strategy now to avoid the worst and maybe even improve your performance.

In SEAL terms, detecting an enemy patrol on the ridgeline represents a threat. If you reposition your team to intercept that threat, then you have an opportunity to surprise them and conduct a successful ambush. Threat equals opportunity.

Many people use threat assessment tools like the SWOT chart—a square with four internal quadrants. The quadrants are strengths, weaknesses, opportunities, and threats. As usual, simple works. The application of SWOT to a particular situation allows you to evaluate your capabilities and limitations against a threat or an opportunity. There are many other tools and software designed to strip and rip potential outcomes, but I like to keep it as easy as possible.

Your evaluation team should use tools like this to collectively score the threat or opportunity. They also should outline recommended actions for you and the business to take, along with a timeline to perform those recommended actions.

In the early 1990s, a rivalry began between the special operations community and the Marine Corps. It was at the height of the drug war, and America was on the offensive, especially in our southern hemisphere. Special operations teams were deployed in Peru, Colombia, and throughout the Caribbean Sea, funded by Congress to stem, if not stop, the flow of drugs into the United States.

Like commercial competition, military organizations often compete for missions and the dollars tied to them. In 1990, this was the case in Venezuela. The Marines saw an opportunity to insert themselves into a new mission category in the region. They started showing up everywhere, pitching their capabilities in counterdrug operations to our allies. This threat was real. If successful, the SEALs and Green Berets could find themselves displaced, out of a mission and the funding that came with it.

I was part of a three-person strategy group evaluating this competitive threat. The chief of naval operations was staying neutral, the Marine hierarchy in Washington, DC, having carried out an effective lobbying campaign already. In the end, we conceived a plan to roll back the gains made by the

Marines by launching multiple briefing teams into the southern hemisphere, to Washington, DC, and to Tampa, Florida, home of the US Special Operations Command.

The messaging was clear and direct. We had the advantage in language skills, we had more advanced riverine and offshore boats, we had better intelligence-gathering assets, and we had more mature operators. It took us six months, but eventually the Marines pulled back and the threat diminished. Your threat evaluation may reveal a problem that requires a more involved and costly response. The sooner your team makes their assessment and presents that assessment to you, the better.

Risk Vs Reward

Return on investment is a calculation many businesses focus on when contemplating a new project, an acquisition, or a new strategy. Your evaluation team also should address the tradeoffs between acting and not acting, in the face of an opportunity or threat. This opportunity cost measure is more difficult to quantify.

Doing nothing may have as much, if not more, risk than doing something. It also may cause you to miss the opportunity of a lifetime. When it's time to assess risk and reward, you'll want to have brain power aligned to that task on your dream team. Again, remember what I said about the difference between the team you assemble to think big thoughts and the team you assemble to evaluate the big thoughts from a practical point of view.

Your evaluation team should run the idea or concept through the wringer, testing your first team's hypothesis. This is a great way to propel a game-changing idea into the early development stage, but also allow for a thorough review of its merits. Allow them to scrutinize the idea before you commit resources or change your strategy.

In for-profit businesses, a return on investment is the point of the exercise. Why risk precious capital, time, and energy only to remain stagnant or tread water? The concept of ROI is often lost on leaders, because it is an investment-oriented metric and not something an employee, manager, or leader would be concerned about.

Entrepreneurs are investors who want to turn one dollar into ten through creation of a new product or service. For these adventurers, ROI is the holy grail. Risk much, or all, and gain greatly. If you are not tuned into ROI at your level of leadership, be assured that the outside or founder investors are certainly watching this measure closely.

Non-profit organizations can benefit from applying an ROI measure and goal for their funded projects. Wasting precious capital is a problem for these folks, too. Address ROI as the reward side of the evaluation equation. Otherwise, you guessed it: all you'll have is a classic risk-focused outcome.

There are many slogans related to risk mitigation crushing dreams. In the mergers and acquisitions industry, it's often said that lawyers kill deals. In the investment industry, the compliance department is referred to as the sales avoidance department. You get the idea. Mitigation is necessary, and it took me a long time to see the value of inviting criticism from those who are trained and psychologically predisposed to saying no.

Defining risk and monetizing risk doesn't necessarily kill the idea. It informs you about what might happen on the downside; and in the end, that is critical information. Lawyers, accountants, and other forms of risk mitigation expertise must be applied to honestly know what you're asking your organization to approve.

From Idea to Business Case

I can't assume you can create stand-alone specialized teams as I've described. If you can, that's great! If not, follow the same process and get at least two other people involved. One to brainstorm the idea and one to evaluate the dream critically.

Now your idea has become a concept with meat attached to the bones

A business concept can be supported by a short and shallow review process or by a much deeper dive. I suggest you put in the time to build your concept into a business case. When I think of this level of presentation, I envision a stern banker, or a panel of unsmiling finance experts, poised to destroy your inspiration by tearing apart the business case associated with the idea. Never assume your concept will be reviewed and approved by friends, supportive colleagues, or cheerful bosses. This is a trap. It lures you into a false sense of success before you've pitched the idea.

It is much better to prepare for war, to have your logic and numbers crosschecked by smart people who are knowledgeable in the areas your concept touches. Preferably this third group were not involved in the prior brainstorming or evaluation phases. It is prudent to invite others to punch holes in the business case before it sees the inside of a conference room.

This is another way to leverage people to assist you in your visionary quest. If your company is small and you lack talent to assist, go outside your business to people you trust. Assume the approval process will be brutal and difficult, every time. This is a recipe for improving your probability of success. I learned all this the hard way.

Mentors were instrumental here. My advisors were mostly senior military leaders who were sympathetic to my struggle to be influential. I was an idea guy early in my professional life. I was also articulate. All of that is fine, but I failed much more often than I succeeded. What I was missing was a development process and a dream team. A group of people who could help me cover all the angles. Experts who could help me bulletproof my idea through rigorous discipline.

In 1979, I was assigned temporarily to a special advanced diving project operating on the campus of Duke University. The project was testing and evaluating a new form of self-contained breathing apparatus or SCUBA device. I was a twenty-one-year-old junior enlisted SEAL at the time. High school educated, with few serious thoughts in my brain. The new SCUBA had a computer inside that anticipated the change in depth as a diver descended.

It had two sources of breathable gas, and you had choices. You could use nitrogen and oxygen, or oxygen and helium. This second mixture was for deep dives, dives below one thousand feet. Our team was comprised of six enlisted SEALs and one officer. I was the second lowest ranking participant on the team.

The project was managed by a civilian PhD who was also a reserve SEAL officer. I asked a lot of questions, and this PhD was nice enough to keep answering them over the five-month project. Near the end, I suspected the cost of maintaining the new SCUBA would be astronomical. The PhD hadn't thought about that aspect of things; he was focused on testing.

One day the PhD called me into his office and slid a piece of paper across his desk toward me. He explained that in the Navy, ideas initially were captured and transmitted to leaders using a one-page concept paper. He went on to explain the format and challenged me to put my concerns about cost and sustained maintenance into words.

I wasn't keen on doing this, but I also wasn't about to say no to a lieutenant commander. I struggled for a few days, then brought my work back to the PhD. For a week he chopped up my logic and my projected outcomes, never answering the questions, just challenging my language and the order of my discourse. Eventually it was completed to his standard.

He congratulated me on a job well done, then tried to convince me to go to college. This would mean night school and take a few years, but he genuinely thought I should become a SEAL officer. I thanked him and walked out of his office. I went back to SEAL Team Two a few weeks later; my time on the Duke University project was over. Four weeks after I returned, I was summoned to the captain's office.

Now, junior enlisted people don't normally have conversations with Navy captains; and if they do, it's never a good thing. When I went in, the executive officer was there, too—double trouble. The captain pointed to a piece of paper on his desk and asked me if I was the author. I stepped forward and recognized my concept paper. I acknowledged I was the source and began to apologize. I was sure I'd angered a bunch of people by being audacious enough to question the advanced SCUBA program in any way. I was wrong.

I was taken to the SEAL commodore's office the next day where I was asked to brief him, my captain, and the captain in charge of Underwater Demolition Team (UDT) Twenty-One. As a result of my paper, the east and west coast SEAL teams would not be accepting the new device. Only the UDT teams would be receiving them. In addition, I was tasked with being the "expert" assigned to UDT Twenty-One to facilitate their acceptance of the new SCUBA.

This was my first professional attempt at making a concept pitch. I was totally unaware of the potential consequences of the paper I produced, but it changed things in a big way. There is no doubt that, without the PhD's help and guidance, I never would have made the suggestions I did in any format. I did, and it changed more than just the advanced diving program.

That learning exercise set me on a course to getting a college degree and eventually to receiving a Navy commission as a SEAL officer. Think about this story when you feel no one is going to listen to your big, bold idea. Gather reinforcements to assist you in crafting the concept into a business case presentation. Use the right talent for each phase of development, and when ready, fire the cannons. If it fails, think big thoughts again and reload on another visionary idea. Don't stop dreaming, don't stop trying, and don't do it all by yourself. Build a dream team!

Chapter Eleven

Pitching the Vision

Every worthwhile accomplishment, big or little, has its stages of drudgery and triumph: a beginning, a struggle and a victory.
Mahatma Gandhi

Corporate vision quests are not as important as saving lives or winning wars, but they are impactful. Just ask anyone who was downsized due to strategic change. To you, as the originator or, at a minimum, the enthusiastic sponsor of a visionary idea, making the pitch to gain approval and resourcing for your strategic project can be daunting, even terrifying. Briefing senior military leaders on your special operations plan of action is a similarly challenging experience.

My mission concept was the combined product of my SEAL operator's input, guided by my direction and insights. Every target or mission is different to some extent, so the mission concept you present is wide open to scorn, shock, and dismissal. This was especially the case for me when I first led SEALs in a combat environment. I was a prior-enlisted SEAL with ten years' service when I received my officer's commission.

My first mission concept brief in combat occurred when I was a lieutenant junior grade, or LTJG, only one step up from the starting rank of ensign. My first audience was General Maxwell Thurman, four-star Army general and commander of Southern Command.

Fail Big

I was trained to prepare a well-organized workflow process briefing, showing the entire series of mission steps, from receipt of tasking to completion of the post-mission intelligence debrief.

In practice, we spent days planning and creating the mission briefing, a briefing that rarely lasted less than two hours. However, the day of truth for LTJG Strong, platoon commander of the sixth platoon, SELA Team Four, wasn't anything like practice.

I was given a mission task and half a day to think it through. This included requesting any, and all, additional support from the Army. My men and I huddled together and pounded out the basic options, eventually settling on the best one based on the intelligence we possessed. There wasn't time to prepare briefing materials as I was whisked away to meet with the general.

General Thurman was famous for destroying briefing officers. I witnessed this firsthand from my place in a long line of briefers, stretched down a wall in a huge briefing room. The general and his staff sat clustered together in chairs facing a white screen. I saw that a few of the officers making presentations tried in vain to set up visual aids, only irritating the general in the process.

As I came closer to the front of the large room, I began to hear the exchanges between the mission briefer and the general. We were a nervous collection of army aviation, infantry, special forces, and mechanized officers. Then there were two stoic looking Marines and me rounding out the mix.

The army ranger officer in front of me went down in flames within a few seconds. His mistake was trying to hold off answering the general's questions until he handed out a mission briefing packet to the small audience. He was cut off mid-sentence and dismissed. Then it was my turn.

I don't remember consciously absorbing the lessons learned as each officer in front of me tried, failed, or succeeded, but I survived. It turns out the general hated PowerPoint and slides, so I was good on that score. I told him my mission number, my mission, and a four-phase concept of operations in less than ninety seconds; then I shut up.

The general looked hard into my eyes and liked what he

saw. He asked one question: "Has my staff provided you with everything you need to be successful?" I nodded my head, rattled off the descriptions of three or four air and ground support teams I had requested and received, then shut up again. We were at the three-minute mark. The general sighed, looked at his watch, and then at the line of officers left to brief him. Without looking back at me, he said, "Approved. Good luck, son."

I've thought about that day hundreds of times over the years, struggling to see what made my pitch acceptable while others failed. I'll share a few of these insights in the rest of this chapter. But the big takeaway is this: the more important the leader, the fewer minutes they must waste on theater. Short, direct, and shut up works every time. No C-level executive wants to sit through a thirty-minute light and color show before reaching the punchline.

The proverbial elevator speech is a myth, but maybe, just maybe, it's the key to pitching a visionary idea to someone who has the power to say yes or no. Let them push you into specifics. Don't oversell with data that clouds the vision and muddies the message. This is a visionary idea. Drive it home with enthusiasm and confidence. That's what sells other visionary decision makers. Let the managers and accountants work out the numbers. Be visionary!

Concept Development

How you approach the development of your concept is critical. If you follow the guidelines and insights presented in the last chapter, then you should be prepared to stand toe-to-toe with the big dogs and pitch away. If you didn't, then you are walking into the pitch session with vulnerabilities. Using the dream team to stretch and flex your initial idea (or the idea you are sponsoring), followed by the critical review team, gives you the Ying and Yang of the idea or concept. It informs you about what is possible on the upside and what may affect or destroy the idea on the downside.

You also can canvass the people who work with and around the key decision maker. Assistants, peers, board members, even social contacts. What are their hot buttons? What are their pain points? What sets them off? Armed with this information, a visionary pitch is ready for the real test. Do those in power agree and see the promise you see?

So, the foundation for success lies in the two-phase assessment of your idea. If you are a leader, then you are required to make decisions and judgments. This is showtime for you. Will you ignore all the upside and take counsel from the critical risk side of the process, or will you ignore risks and wrap your arms around the sunny upside in its entirety, without reservations? Will you split the baby and take insight from both to exercise compromise? I suggest both are wrong.

The first is naive and silly. Ignoring information you don't agree with isn't intelligent. The second isn't bold, courageous, or rational. If the dosage requires ten units, and after discussing the merits with others you all agree to make the dosage five units, then the patient won't improve. The requirement is ten units. Compromise often results in excellence being diluted.

Compromise isn't an objective in business; it's a conflict avoidance behavior. When Steve Jobs told his engineers at Apple that he wanted them to make a smart phone the size of a pack of cigarettes, he didn't listen to their pushback and decide to appease their lack of faith or vision by agreeing to make it bigger.

Compromise works when the parties do not have the same objectives. Diplomacy requires compromise for this very reason. Countries have differing strategies and are rightly self-serving. Compromise in diplomacy prevents wars and builds alliances. Within a business organization, there should not be differing strategies and objectives for the company. These should be pounded out, decided, and pursued.

If I lived in New York City and my vacation to Disney World

in Orlando was open to compromise, the result might be a vacation destination halfway to Florida. So, when you divine the work product of your dream and critical assessment teams, use your brain to see the right path. Decide regarding that path and then, as they say in the Navy, move forward smartly!

A few years ago, I realized my healthcare company was growing so fast we would not be able to fund the growth organically. We needed an infusion of borrowed capital to keep pace or slow that pace to what was affordable and within our means to support. The demand signal from the market was staggering. We were sitting on over twenty unfulfilled healthcare corporation prospects, closed, and waiting to have our services begin immediately.

We didn't advertise or market our capabilities, nor did we have salespeople. We didn't need any help getting the business. I spoke to several internal leaders to determine what we might need. I allowed myself to lean to the conservative side because of their input and my reluctance to fully embrace the trend we were experiencing. I pitched our private equity backer for additional capital and cited the backlog. I asked for one million dollars.

The response was classic, "Why are you so pessimistic about the future? This trend and the backlog would require more than one million dollars. Go back and create a projection over the next three years, estimate your working capital shortfall to execute, and then come back and pitch us for the full amount to achieve strategic success."

In this example, I wasn't bold or audacious. I whittled the ask down until it appeared reasonable and affordable for the private equity firm. I learned as I became more experienced that the bigger the ask, the more likely a leader will hedge and compromise the dream. Asking for five million dollars or ten million dollars sounds much less likely to succeed than compromising down to a two or three million dollar ask.

Be bold in your evaluation of the concept post-development.

The insights may prove your idea is a dud or a game changer, but read those tea leaves objectively and honestly, as a leader. You are not a diplomat; you are not an ambassador for happiness. You are a leader, and being a leader goes hand-in-hand with the risk of failure. Once you are past the two phases of development and assessment, decide and prepare to pitch the idea.

Core Deliverable—Threat or Opportunity

To reflect on the beginning of this book, it's important to remember the visionary insight you present may not be a good-news story. There are many clichés found in popular end-of-the-world movies that depict scientists, theologians, and government leaders coming to grips with a calamity (a super asteroid impact is my favorite movie threat). In practice this group crisis decision-making rarely happens. Think President John F. Kennedy during the 1962 Cuban Missile Crisis. There is an iconic picture of him alone pondering the awesome responsibilities of his duties. The worse the crisis is, the more the final call falls on the top leader.

You may be pitching three things when it comes to potential threats. First, you may have to identify the threat if it isn't apparent or easily recognized. Second, you may have to assign consequence or adverse impact on the business to the identified threat. And third, you may have to pitch the solution.

There are times when you alone will know enough to present the threat but not enough to ascribe financial consequences or time and resources to have a threat response plan ready to pitch. When it comes to threats, this is perfectly acceptable. Better to say you spotted the planet-killing asteroid as soon as possible, rather than wait until your pitch is fully supported by a deliberate and possibly long-concept development effort.

Opportunities are a bit different. Senior decision makers and capital resource entities (private equity, banks, venture capital firms, etc.) will not feel compelled to take your visionary idea and run with it. Not without an answer to "Why?" The "why" in a threat pitch often is compelling enough to act as a catalyst for action. "The asteroid is coming! Enough said. All hands on deck and let's figure this out quick!"

That is rarely the response you will get when pitching strategic opportunity, for obvious reasons. Another lesson I learned from my experience pitching to General Thurman was that there is a good chance the person you are pitching to is in that job because they know how to think in visionary terms. In fact, they may spend a good portion of their day contemplating contingencies related to both distant threats and opportunities.

This is why I strongly suggest you hit the audience with the punchline and shut up. There's a high probability the senior leader will immediately extend the logic of your punchline into the future, bounce it against all alternatives and prior opinions, and arrive side-by-side with you as an energetic supporter—all within thirty seconds or so.

Interestingly, threats often have a flipside for those who see the threat early and act. There is more to taking decisive action than playing defense. For example, if you knew your core business of making products was threatened with extinction by a new technology, then you could become an early adopter of that same technology or develop your own version. Shifting the core business in a deliberate and accelerated strategy is one possible course of action.

You could also retool the business to become a service provider to the industry instead of making the product. Pierre Dupont, a billionaire entrepreneur in the early twentieth century, was adept at seeing the end of one wave and the beginning of the next. Over the course of several decades, his business infrastructure went from being an ammunition maker, to buying and expanding a fledgling General Motors car company, to making household products. Your vision doesn't have to be focused solely on the doom and gloom aspect of your insight.

Then there's the classic human reaction to opportunity. When you make your vision pitch, you will be painting a future that will terrify those who are comfortably invested in the status quo, many of them leaders, maybe even the top decision maker. Switching from people to software? Physical to virtual? Organic ownership of resources to a gig economy model of transient experts? It is important to have the situational awareness to understand one person's opportunity is another's personal and professional threat.

I'm telling you this so you are aware that the second your idea is out in the open, people in your organization will vilify you and start a countercampaign to kill the initiative. Don't allow this to deter you from thinking big or from boldly pitching the dream or threat concept. As I've said, visionary leaders require courage.

Structuring the Pitch

I frequently share an experience I had in the early days of my time as a financial advisor. I was contacted by phone by an older man requesting that I meet with him to discuss his investments. This was a voicemail that included an invitation to have the meeting at his son's seafood restaurant. I decided to meet the stranger for lunch the next day, because I had ten or so clients and was scrambling to find business.

The lunch went surprisingly well. He didn't want to talk about money; he was an old World War II Navy commando officer. The Scouts and Raiders were a tiny, specialized unit in the Pacific theater and a precursor to today's modern SEAL teams. He was aware of my military background through an article I'd written, and that was the gist of his initial interest in me. I left the two-hour lunch exhausted from answering questions about SEALs and frustrated at wasting so much time without any business benefit.

I received a call from the man a few days later, and he asked me to come to his house and meet with his wife and him to review their investments. I asked several questions, which he graciously answered, and agreed to make the presentation at his house the next week. When the moment of truth came, I was nervous. At this point, I'd been out of uniform for five months, most of that studying for and taking all the finance licensing exams.

The gentleman had revealed that his estate was worth somewhere around four to six million dollars and consisted of multiple investments. I spent several days preparing my presentation. On the day of the meeting, I dragged an easel and large multipage display into the couple's dining room. I was wearing a five-hundred-dollar suit and was as ready as I'd ever been for any SEAL mission briefing.

I started by showing them the federal estate tax table. Over the phone, the man told me he didn't have a will or a trust in place. I handed them each a copy of the table, where I'd highlighted their likely estate tax obligation, should they pass without a will or more complicated measures in place. I began to reveal the next page in my display, but was stopped by a gruff voice saying, "You're a liar!"

I've edited the actual expletives used in his sentence, but it was alarming to say the least. It also was the best thing that ever happened to me in the investment business, because I wasn't used to being challenged or insulted like that. My Navy SEAL came out, and I stared him down before speaking.

When I did open my mouth, I began by aggressively telling him he was wrong and then pounded out what was going to happen to the wealth they'd accumulated over fifty years when the IRS swooped in and took their share. I told them that a little more than fifty percent of their six-million-dollar estate wasn't going to their kids or to their grandkids. It was going to the government.

I was standing, leaning forward; and as I finished, I relaxed and regained my composure. They were silent. I then felt a wave of regret. The man's wife was a sweet older lady, and she didn't deserve hearing my retort delivered in such a crude manner. I turned to flip the next page to get into asset diversification, asset allocation, risk models based on asset class, etc., but stopped when I heard that gruff voice again. "Like I used to tell my salesmen: when you've made the sale, shut the hell up!"

I didn't have to present the rest of my information that day. He became my first high-net-worth client and a future referral source for a dozen additional wealthy clients. Deliver the punchline and shut up; you might be surprised with the results!

Pitch Support Team

If the vision is going to be controversial or require large expenditures of capital, expect a focus on details. Most leaders or managers are either strategy- or detail-oriented. The strategy-oriented leader will hear your presentation and either see the light or not. If they see the vision, then they will know that the details are the next step and not relevant to the pitch.

If they are detail-oriented, they will immediately ask for the supporting data that convinced you it was worth wasting their time. It's not always the case that detail-focused decision makers are really focused on risk, but it is a possibility. The old risk versus gain formula, return on investment, what's in it for me?

Detail people can also be excited and hope the details you provide don't undermine your thesis. In either case, there is only so much expertise you as the leader making the pitch can personally represent. That's why you need a pitch support team.

In the 1990s, SEALs (and special operations units in general) were in high demand. Every major warfighting staff around the world wanted a SEAL on their staff. SEALs were being incorporated into more and more military exercises, too. This created a dilemma nobody had anticipated. SEAL officers were young, much younger than the military staffs they joined or briefed.

Twenty-four-year-olds were interacting with professionals from the Navy and other services, who were in their mid- to late thirties. Our officers were also junior in rank. The combination of these two factors might be disconcerting, but a third factor was the nail in the coffin.

Our officers didn't know how to pitch a mission concept to senior decision makers. Our peers did. They incorporated concept planning and pitch delivery into their junior officer training on day one. We needed to address this as a military unit, and we did.

In 1991, a two-star general sent a personal note to our SEAL admiral addressing this shortfall. He'd been observing a major exercise and witnessed firsthand our SEAL officers floundering and flailing. The general didn't blame the young officers; he blamed our senior leadership for sending them out untutored and ill-prepared. I received a call to attend a meeting on the subject; and when that meeting was over, I'd been tasked with fixing the problem.

We had a junior officer course that focused on administration and how to do Navy paperwork. The officers could attend if they wanted to; it wasn't mandatory. I designed a new junior officer course that directly answered the concerns expressed in the general's note. My design was approved, along with my recommendation that all officers graduating basic SEAL training be required to go through the new junior officer course after graduating the basic SEAL selection course and before leaving for their new SEAL Team assignments.

Why was I selected to fix this problem? Well, for one thing, I ended up briefing many more senior leaders after that tense meeting with General Thurman in Panama. I briefed General Colin Powell, then the Chairman of the Joint Chiefs of Staff; I briefed Senator Sam Nunn, Chair of the Armed Services Committee; I even briefed Dick Chaney, then the Secretary of Defense. I was the most experienced junior officer pitchman the admiral had close at hand, so I was given the task to fulfill.

So, I built and supervised the course. A key element of my personal winning formula during my combat tour was to bring several of my technical-expert enlisted SEALs with me when I conducted mission briefings. I never relied on my memory to recall specialized details and making up answers was a career-ending mistake.

In practice, my support team would sit quietly, listening to my pitch until someone requested a detail or technical answer. I didn't always use them; but when I did, it was impactful. The person asking the detailed question was rarely an expert either. The support team of smart SEALs were part of my pitch preparations, and we'd rehearsed the flow of questions and answers, including how I would hand off to them.

They spoke, stopped, and waited for the next cue from me. Often people stopped asking detail questions, because it was clear my team were experts, were part of the concept development, and they had my back. I suggest you bring a pitch support team with you when it's showtime. It's great to have even one person—a financial planning or analysis expert familiar with the upside or downside consequences—in your back pocket. As the Boy Scouts say, be prepared.

Pitch the Vison and Shut Up

I don't believe in complex formats as a rule. Think elevator speech and you'll see why. No one important has the time or patience to wait for your opening monologue to get to the point. "Sir, I want to marry your daughter." This is a great way to get a father's attention, right? Think direct and to the point. The art of presentation, as taught conventionally, isn't structured to win; it's structured to be a crutch for average people to get through the stress of the presentation.

The formats and fancy graphs are a corporate form of whistling in a haunted house. They don't make the pitch better, only longer and more confusing. "Sir, RADAR shows three squadrons of enemy bombers inbound, two hundred miles out. At their current speed they will be here in forty-five minutes." Is anybody going to ask what color the bombers are? Of course not. Getting the attention of senior decision makers isn't an art; it's easy. Think elevator speech, and your vision has a chance of taking wing!

Chapter Twelve

Strategy is the Enemy of Optimization

Thousands of great ideas cannot make you successful, but better execution of just one idea can change your life.
Nitin Namdeo

Optimization has been a popular sport for corporate business for decades. First led by financial engineers, then by supply chain gurus, and finally by techies, optimization has become the holy grail of effective management theory. The concept of lean operations, raised by efficient Japanese car production in the 1970s and 1980s, challenged American industries to trim the fat, streamline linear production, automate manual functions, and measure efficiencies on a micro scale. It's ironic that these concepts were originally introduced to post World War II Japan by American engineer and statistician W. Edwards Deming.

Deming's insights were logical and straightforward. He'd observed the amazing ascent of American wartime manufacturing power from 1942 to 1945 and saw examples of ever-increasing efficiency, while scaling upwards in greater and greater industrial capacity. America was a rural society before World War II. Linear analysis of the step-by-step process of making a product allowed management to tighten up timelines, reduce and eliminate waste (time, space, and money), and achieve a higher level of productivity, at scale, and with a high degree of quality control. Deming's influence is still felt in the United States today.

There were countless private industry leaders and influencers of enlightened manufacturing after World War II. A global war that saw destruction on a scale never experienced in human history. Military might on every side of the conflict made use of all the power of science and industry available to level cities, decimate populations, and mangle industrial capabilities.

Despite this sad reality, the 1950s post-war world experienced a renaissance in business thinking. This occurred naturally in the United Kingdom, Germany, Italy, France, and across Europe—anywhere societies faced the choice of rebuilding their former economic glory or watching their proud cultures fade into obscurity.

Open-minded business visionaries arose who understood the opportunity of starting anew while most perceived only ruin. In the ensuing post-war years, these economies were rebuilt, gained traction, and then accelerated their momentum in production capacity, quality execution, and efficiency.

This was not the case in the United States. While Deming's insights were based on the miracle of American manufacturing in the 1940s and 1950s, the American post-war experience didn't result in revolutionary concepts in production efficiency. America was not bombed and devasted by the global war. Her production capabilities heading into the 1960s reflected both pre-war and wartime factory functional design and manufacturing mindsets.

America became the world's leading economy because of being spared the widespread destruction, and therefore it had no compelling reason to change. It would take global competition in the 1970s, from an ascending Japan and other European economies, to wake up American business. America's lethargy had resulted in a culture of consumerism and consumption.

Mass production was easy for a country that had made more bombers, tanks, and ships than any other nation in the four years of World War II. During the 1960s, American manufacturing made fun of Japan's attempts to break out, turning the phrase "Made in Japan" into a running joke. But the Japanese were learning.

From the 1970s onward, American industries watched, one-by-one, as global competitors wooed their consumers from homemade to foreign-made products. This wasn't a price war; this was a quality war.

American cars and trucks in the 1970s were unreliable, they burned gasoline inefficiently, and they were ugly. The difference was so stark that a new post-war generation of Baby Boomer Americans ignored the anti-Japanese attitudes of their parents and were happily choosing Japanese cars and loving the experience.

This was a black swan moment for the US auto industry. And as with most black swan experiences, the big three automakers began by ignoring the threat, denying quality was the issue, and then finally saw it was time to retool and catch up. The Japanese and European competition was also impacting household goods, appliances, and a whole range of consumer products in America. It was time for American industry to become humble, to realize that they were in a fistfight and they were losing.

America did figure it out, and by the 1990s, the country was a leader in quality manufacturing once again. The global competition didn't go away, but America was in the fight to win consumer loyalty. A fight defined by quality. This short history lesson in twentieth century competition is important because it illuminates the hubris often associated with success and demonstrates that failure, even on a global scale, can be overcome by those who are willing and able to see opportunity in the ashes.

To seize opportunity and come back swinging. Optimization and quality control often are seen as the same business objective; but in practice, especially since the early twenty-first century, optimization has become more about stripping cost and operating as lean as possible and not an unrelenting focus on quality.

The subtitle to this book is *Strategic Leadership in the Age of Optimization*. We will continue to circle back to the vision development process and leading dramatic change; but in this chapter, I want to share with you my insights on where optimization is today as a best practice and why I believe it is choking off visionary and strategic thinking.

Optimization Is Not Evil

First off, I'm a fan of operational and technical optimization. Performed for the right reasons, optimization efforts take one thing, analyze inputs and throughputs, and then make intelligent adjustments to improve outputs. It works on processes and systems that do not involve human beings. It is less successful once we get involved. Our emotions, needs, wants, moods, objectives, and fears all conspire to "gum up the works," so to speak.

Athletes work hard to optimize their physical and mental performance, and it works. In business, optimization routinely misses the value and criticality of the human-machine (process, system) interface and instead focuses on the things that are easy to measure, monitor, and analyze. Human behavior is designed to be inconsistent; therefore, we frustrate optimization specialists time and time again.

My professional beef with the way optimization is championed in business today is simple. When I see optimization specialists, usually financial professionals, extend optimization into strategy and vision development, I shudder. It feels like a person attempting to paint a Picasso using only straight lines and right angles. That is good for building construction, but hardly inspiring.

In the last twenty years, publicly traded companies in the United States have first augmented, and then nearly replaced C-suite salaries with stock options. This shift in compensation theory was based on good intentions. C-level salaries were rising at an incredible rate, and companies needed to stem the trend and the growing disparity between what leaders were paid and those employees doing the productive work, day in and day out. Stock options put the leaders in a symbiotic relationship with the shareholders. Grow the value and the share price rises. If the senior business leaders are successful, then everyone wins.

Yet, there are many ways to increase stock value. You can stop paying cash dividends. You can use cash to buy back the stock, creating fewer shares and pushing prices higher. You can trim costs and, here it comes, optimize operations to achieve maximum leanness. Lean is smart and lean increases the margins, which in turn increases stock prices.

So far, so good. Right? Maybe not. Here's the punch line. There are a few more things a company can do to expand margins and push short-term stock prices higher. They can cut research and development, growth by making acquisitions, they can reduce marketing and advertising budgets. They can forego market expansion plans, let sales staff go, and trim back on product promotion. These little extras will contribute to even bigger margins, and the stock price will climb.

Leaders Are People and People Lead Companies

When I was in the investment advice business, I was what is called a value investor. My clients at UBS were aware of my style of money management; and if it aligned with their goals and risk tolerance, we meshed. If not, I asked them to find an advisor who did. I refrained from studying stock charts like they were astrology calculations, a form of divining the future referred to as quantitative investing.

I adhered to great value-focused mutual fund managers of the 1990s like Peter Lynch, who led the Fidelity's Magellan Fund, and Bill Miller of Legg Mason Value Trust fame. Value-based investing looks at the business performance numbers—they are important—but it also goes further. I learned how to evaluate the competitive tradeoff between companies in the same markets and industries. Why was one doing well and the others not so much? Frequently the answer to the question was management and what management was doing or not doing about the future.

There's a reflection on the future and the intensity of challenges that goes like this: delay the important and it eventually becomes urgent. Delay the urgent and it becomes an emergency. Management teams who ignored the market feedback, product sales numbers, or the direction of innovation in their lane, did so at their peril.

The length of time from when something's important to when it becomes urgent varies from industry to industry. High technology compresses success and failure. You need to immediately "embrace the suck," charge into a new vision, and then implement that vision, pronto!

In more classic manufacturing, such as cars, trucks, and furniture, management may have more time to pontificate and tread water. But the change it is a-coming, and they too will lead themselves into an emergency by their apathetic response to the urgent truth.

I saw this repeatedly, in company after company. It was a human thing. Agnostic as to product or service, market or industry. People are arrogant or fearful, even leaders. Procrastination and delays are normal behaviors. The abnormal management teams seized upon the truth and took swift action, even if the opportunity or threat they perceived was years away.

It was clear to me that while I was not a quant (a wizard with advance analysis of numbers), I was a student of human nature and especially leadership behavior. The way these management teams were acting made perfect sense to me, even early in my investment management career. Our internal quantitative analysts provided me with the numbers and their opinions on what the numbers meant.

I then added my analysis of corporate leadership and steerage. I soon began to see the difference between a Warren

Buffet, buying great companies led by great management teams for his Berkshire Hathaway fund, and my peers who were buying and selling based primarily on short-term number performance.

In a strange parallel, I realized companies that had not been truly challenged for many years took on certain traits. Practical certain behaviors, repetitive behaviors. Behavior that remained unchallenged for so long they evolved into traditions. While I was in the SEAL Teams, there was a period after 1972 when the Vietnam was over and combat missions were rare.

The veterans of that conflict were fond of experimentation. They changed tactics (think football, basketball, or soccer plays) many times over the decade SEALs fought in Vietnam. When I joined, I was trained by these jungle warriors, and they taught me flexibility, agility, and creativity when it came to tactics.

They taught me that anything might work for a while—that is until the enemy adapted. When that happened, it was time for the SEALs to adapt, too. This made sense at the time. However, the years passed without a new war to confirm the logic of those early adopters in special warfare. We began to embrace traditions, and soon the traditions became law.

In speaking with SEALs who went into Iraq or Afghanistan after the September 2001 attacks on the World Trade Center and the Pentagon, I realized they too had succumbed to tradition in the years after Operation Urgent Fury in Grenada, Operation Just Cause in Panama, Desert Storm, and other smaller flareups prior to the beginning of the new millennium.

Until the invasion of Grenada, we practiced tactical maneuvers and footwork, codified and sacred, in response to unimaginative attacks, usually from a distinct direction (left, right, front, and rear). Once SEALs went into harm's way again, the folly of this training emphasis on tradition and preplanned choreography was revealed.

Creative adaptiveness and agile thinking were again confirmed in battle as the intelligent way to fight. The enemy always had a plan, too, and they rarely attacked "from the left." As I grew to become a seasoned investment professional, I took these human lessons to heart and became more successful picking market leaders and winners as a result.

Strategy Is the Enemy of Optimization

For many years after I left UBS, these observations were reinforced everywhere I worked as a member of senior management. I sought to influence thinking and decision-making by constantly applying what I'd observed in top management teams across the country as a student of what worked and what didn't.

The problem, of course, was people. People have opinions, and different memories, education, and tendencies. They also have a tendency for petty jealousy, paranoia, and corporate maneuvering for promotion. These were all in play until I became a CEO (more on that dynamic later). I found it hard to influence the other management team members. Hard to paint a picture of the truth and convince them to respond to that truth.

During those years, I wasn't always successful in using my UBS knowledge, but it was worth trying. I always cared about the greater good and well-being of the companies I worked for, and it felt natural to want the collective team to avoid calamity and seize opportunities.

I've concluded at this point in my career that strategy is the enemy of optimization. I say this because of the average leader's adverse reaction to the idea of looking out into the unknown. It is immediate and uniform. Strategy is great, but we have work to do now. We can discuss strategy later, maybe next week, next month, maybe never.

I understand why they react this way. Strategy is someday thinking, and optimization is real-time thinking. Optimization shows tangible benefits, quickly. Strategy takes time to prove out. It is not an exact science. Data mining historical references to decide what to do in the short-term is the new way of business. Strategy is now understood to be the perpetuation of incremental daily and weekly improvements. Actions crosschecked with the past to ensure that few mistakes in judgment will be made.

Optimization is based on the reality of numbers and risk mitigation, while strategy is all smoke and mirrors. Soothsaying and voodoo dreams. Prophecy isn't even an elective in America's top MBA programs. Efficiency is noble and optimization is virtuous but seeing into the future and anticipating change is how humanity advances. It's how businesses advance. Leaders and companies ignore strategy at their peril.

Have you experienced this? Are you currently in an organization that focuses on the elimination of errors instead of sponsoring bright new outlooks? Error and risk are everywhere; I understand that is true. However, so is opportunity. Dreaming big is difficult to do in an organization steeped in linear projections of the past and tight optimization of the status quo. Consider the following example.

If I took my retirement savings in 2011 and put it all in Tesla stock, I would've been perceived as a fool. At the time, Tesla was a six-dollar stock led by a man most thought to be delusional, Elon Musk. He was not what Wall Street considered to be bankable, because all he did was dream and speak about his dreams. Ten years later, my crazy bet on his dreams would have secured my retirement for many years to come. Yet in 2011, there was no track record, no data to mine or numbers to roll forward with confidence.

Business entities that approach challenges and the future like Tesla, will never wow us by adhering to optimization as a strategy. Instead, they are led by dreamers and draw hope, inspiration, and talent to them as they begin to go vertical. While visionary leadership is valuable and, alas, rare, you can learn to be visionary.

Optimizing a Bad Strategy Results in Failure

Another thing to consider, as we compare optimized versus strategic leadership, is the quality of the strategy that is in place now. I've discussed how compromising on strategy can set you up for a surprise when the consequences of a watered-down response come home to roost in real time. Bad strategies exist. In fact, most "strategies" are not strategies at all. They are linear projections of current and recent performance modeled out into the future.

This is silly as it ignores the universe, a universe filled with lions and tigers and bears, oh my! In nature we don't expect a tree to grow until it touches the moon, based on historical data projected forward year after year. We recognize trees have limits to their growth. Companies also have growth limits. A tree cannot evolve into a fish as a tactic to change its limited growth destiny; but a company can do this, and it should.

Here we can contemplate the combination of a shortsighted, compromised business strategy enabled by highly efficient optimization. Optimizing a bad plan doesn't make up for a plan's faults, and it may even exacerbate them. This is usually not a disconnect observed by optimizers. They have a mission, and that mission is sacred and good.

Get lean, get clean, and beat the last set of data points on your way to excellence in minute execution. Meanwhile, a competitor is two months from rolling out a new product or service that directly answers the market's demand for something better, and you're stunned. You just didn't see it coming. Optimization experts, brought into strategic planning or to reflect on the success of the strategy, apply what they do and ensure a tighter execution of the current plan, not a new plan.

To honestly review an existing strategy, you need to fall back on the two-phase approach I covered in an earlier chapter. Let the dream team stretch, pull, poke, and bench test the underlying hypothesis of the existing plan to discover shortsightedness, namely a lack of intuitive insights (threats and opportunities on the horizon). Let them shape a possible future for the organization instead of reliance on a linear expectation.

After they are finished, bring in the critical thinkers. Let them have a shot at the strategy as it sits today and the dreamer's work product. You notice I don't suggest the classic management review, consisting of committees staffed with the very same people who created the compromise and shortsighted plan in the first place. Then present the approved continuation, revision, or overhaul of the organization's strategy in an energized pitch session.

Do not rubber stamp strategy as, "Something we'll figure out when we get there." Address it fresh each time and challenge the earlier assumptions vigorously. If it holds up, great! If not—

When Do You Toss Out the Plan?

This is a painful experience. Especially if you are wedded to a plan that was on target for a year or so, only to have the universe change things up on you. Over time, leaders become comfortable with their plans. They begin to defend their work more and more, intimidating thought leaders and visionaries into silence. Peers and coworkers see something isn't quite right but are not asked to weigh in with senior leadership.

My first book, *Be Nimble,* was all about being humble as a prelude to agile and nimble thinking. Open-minded learning and seeking out oblique information and data points requires this humility. Evaluating a strategy does, too. So, what do you do if you realize the plan isn't working?

A special operations warrior or Marine rifleman would answer immediately with, "Improvise, adapt, and overcome." Sounds simple, and it is simple. When the plan isn't working, stop and craft a new plan.

Human nature isn't so simple, however. People tend to hold on to the plan and expect or predict something will happen to bring it back on target. There's always an outside chance they're correct, but it rarely happens.

Post black swan analysis usually points to leadership's unwillingness to accept the new reality and act. This refusal to be honest and adaptable is rampant among business leaders in America. It is difficult to face the music, as they say; but leaders, good leaders, great leaders, know they have only one choice and that is to *lead*.

Don't toss out the entire strategic plan until you've run the two phases I showed you. Being overly reactive can lead to hyper planning, and overthinking everything all the time is just as destructive as lethargic strategic leadership. Run the review process. Test the assumptions. Keep what still applies, toss out what doesn't. Lay out a timeline to take decisive action, resource the new vision, fire up the optimization team, and execute!

As a team, optimization and strategy can work in harmony to achieve greatness. Pursued separately and in a vacuum, they can tug and pull the company off the road and into a ditch. Being visionary is challenging; but as you can see, there is a method to the madness!

Chapter Thirteen

Making the Aspirational Actionable

Plans are only good intentions unless they immediately degenerate into hard work.
Peter F. Drucker

Congratulations! You've convinced the boss, the CEO, and the banks that your vision is credible and worthy of support and resourcing. Up to this point, I've emphasized a leader's character and passion in the pursuit of new opportunities or in the avoidance of looming threats. However, when it comes to implementation, it's a team sport all the way.

This is where a well-designed battle plan, well executed, can make your dream, the collective dream, come true. This also is where optimization is a good thing, if you don't allow the desire to perfect the art of sharpening pencils to become the default goal over time. Your task now is to select the team, its leaders, and to review their plan of action. Once the plan is approved, you need to be vigilant against strategic drift and play the role of cheerleader.

The longer a plan takes to achieve the strategic aims, the harder it will be to stay the course and remember the point of the original exercise. You are the one who must keep the flame burning; you are the one who must remind the team why change is vital to the survival or continued success of the organization.

Subtle Shifts in Strategy

So far, I've addressed strategic adjustments in grand terms. Big sweeping changes that drive people crazy, inspire fear, and cause confusion and even retrenchment in the old ways as a defensive reaction. Your vision doesn't have to be radical. In fact, it may be that most visionary changes require more subtle course adjustments instead of structural overhauls. There will still be anxiety and concern about the future (felt by each employee affected), but this should be nominal and easily moderated with clear communications and steady leadership.

I suggest you follow the same evaluation and analysis process described in earlier chapters to ensure that a subtle change is all that is required. Create a solid pitch and take it as seriously as a major strategic shift. Sell the vision and outline the timeline, but don't get tricked into throwing out a half-baked plan during the initial pitch. Take this one premeditated bite at a time.

Another pitfall, when it comes to subtle changes, is a lack of awareness that the subtle maneuver is still a critical one. People instinctively understand a major change is dramatic, costly, disruptive, and therefore must be inherently justified. The boss or bosses wouldn't put us through all this unless it was important, right?

A slight tweak or shift in course may be perceived as ho-hum, not deserving of high energy and attention. You must watch for this apathy closely and continuously through the project implantation process. If you are working your strategic change through subordinate leaders and managers, then watch them closely, too.

People are not always consistent over time, and personalities can create disjointed adherence to your master plan. Let them know you are watching and request frequent feedback on progress or hiccups. Show your face to the team periodically to reinforce that you are paying attention and that the plan is important.

Missteps in Military Strategy

I've noted before that when I entered the SEAL teams, the population was all jungle fighters. The Navy knew full well Vietnam was over and that other threats were looming around the world, as the Cold War between the Soviet Union and the United States challenged global stability. Two strategic initiatives were implemented to deal with this atmosphere. First, SEALs were going to become qualified in sinking enemy combat ships; and second, they were going to become arctic warriors.

These two critical additions to the list of mission capabilities were strategically inspired somewhere in the Pentagon. But by the time the changes trickled down to each SEAL unit, the rationale for change was either diluted or lost. The order to change wasn't wrapped in strategic logic or reason, it was just an order. Trust me, this caused a lot of hate and discontent at the troop level.

Learning how to sink a ship requires learning how to dive for long periods of time under water and navigate using a simple compass and time calculations. We didn't know where to start. Eventually we tapped into German and French special operators, who were in our command on an exchange program.

These two units were adept at advanced ship attack techniques and tactics. They also had advanced SCUBA rebreathing rigs that worked. Our American version was developed in 1958 and leaked like a sieve. The great push into this new capability wasn't going to happen until we received the resources to execute. This was the same case with arctic warfare training.

As mentioned, we were trained to operate in the jungle. Light, lean, stealthy. Cross country skiing with one hundred and ten pounds on our backs wasn't ninja-like at all. In this situation, we turned to two British commandos, also on loan to the United States. They were Royal Marines first and had spent a lot of time on skis and in the arctic environment during their careers.

This learning curve was more painful than learning how to attack enemy ships. There was no specialized equipment for our first foray into the Canadian wilderness; and what we borrowed from the Canadians was heavy, ill-fitting, and designed for sentry duty, not long-distance skiing. We had Boy Scout pup tents, a few stoves, and World War II era wooden skis. Once again, a strategic shift had not been thought out and resourced.

It took us several years to achieve the shift to these two new warfighting areas, but it could've been accomplished in half the time with far less pain and failure. To be fair, during this time in Navy history, there were no SEAL admirals and no fancy SEAL staffs dedicated to thinking big thoughts. Those structures and institutions were established in later years to deal with the disconnect between the big Navy and the Pentagon.

In retrospect, the casual nature of this order, and the lofty expectation that the required strategic shift would simply happen, provide a great lesson in visionary planning, resourcing, oversight, and follow-through. Don't underestimate the challenges and stay on top of the demands the changes have created. This will help you lead through the choke points and be successful, even in pursuit of subtle changes.

Making Bigger Changes

When subtle adjustments won't fit the bill, it may be time to make bigger changes, significant transitions from what and how things are being done. From 2003 to 2014, the War on Terror spurred an incredible demand for private sector services and staffing power. The military drawdown and base closure efforts during the 1990s created the so-called "peace dividend." A strategy that backfired nine months into the next decade, when America was attacked by global terrorists.

The nation went to war and found they were short on almost everything required to fight one. This generated a drive to contract support services of every kind, something not seen since World War II. In February of 2009, I joined a small training company focused on training the Navy's security professionals. The founder had won a lucrative five-year contract and wasn't willing to be a one-hit wonder. That's where I came into the picture.

I joined the small company and took inventory. All our revenue was derived from one service line: training. We only had one customer, the United States Navy. This was the very definition of concentration risk. When I'd managed money, we always were being reminded to beware of closing the elephant and becoming complacent as a result.

An elephant is a big client, and in those days that was defined by someone with over a million dollars in assets, ready to be invested. Sitting on a great contract might lead to some defense contractors relaxing, but not this founder. I worked on an analysis of the sectors within the federal market, assessed opportunities for us to grow, and developed a strategy that might allow us to survive and expand. I called this strategy "the pivot."

We implemented the pivot strategy in early 2010. It was simple—by 2013, our revenue must come from the Department of Defense as well as other federal agencies. A fifty-fifty division in revenue sourcing. In addition, we were required to achieve the same split in service lines. Half of our contracts by revenue from training, and half our revenue from anything but training.

We knew the larger war was going to scale down and our overreliance on the Department of Defense, and specifically the Navy, made us vulnerable. When I explained the new pivot strategy to the managers and employees for the first time, there was a confused silence.

The logic was simple, and the potential threat was clear. What they couldn't grasp instinctively was what, if any, impact the new strategy would have on them, professionally and, of course, personally. Since the question wasn't asked, I took a deep breath and began to explain the execution plan to achieve the strategic aims.

The company had to maintain management oversight of the existing contract work, handle compliance and human resources challenges, seek to win any recompete of existing business, and in addition, double all business development efforts focused on new customers and new service lines. After I stopped speaking, I saw the lights coming on. One-by-one the expressions on their faces changed—some happy, some still pensive, and only a few worried. It was a lot to ask of a small team.

We had nine employees in our management team at the time, and I was asking them to do the work of twice that number. I explained to them we couldn't expand the team until we began to win new contracts, that was the chicken and the egg reality. To their credit, all nine rogered up for the challenge and leaned forward.

To begin with, we had to cross-train everybody in everybody's contract management and business development function. By the time we achieved our strategic goal, on schedule in 2013, we'd all become experts in at least four critical skill sets or knowledge categories. Including me and the founder.

It was all hands on deck, all the time. Subtle strategic change doesn't require this amount of vigor and repurposing. It is actionable, achievable, and a constant contact sport to make large-scale strategic change a success. Then there's the vison and strategy that requires a complete makeover.

Flipping It All on Its Head

Financial management came into its own, at least for the masses, in the mid-1990s. Until then most major brokerage houses focused on selling products, namely stocks and bonds until the late 1960s and then mutual funds. My first branch manager was a product of the period known as the go-go sixties. A time when the economy was roaring, and the market saw a steady stream of companies bringing technology to the consumer market.

Futuristic names for companies driving the growth were all the rage, companies like Telex, Control Data, Teledyne, and Texas Instruments. The Haloid Company had been around since 1906; but they too jumped into the name game, rebranding themselves as Xerox. I joined the industry in January 1996 and expected to be trained in how to find prospects, pitch the features and benefits on a company-generated stock or bond list, and achieve financial success through volume of sales over time. I was wrong.

I entered the profession when two sea changes were about to disrupt the world of investing. The first was the decision by Merrill Lynch to model themselves after J.P. Morgan's high-net-worth client model, focusing on estate planning and asset capture instead of retail sales to retail clients.

The second was the introduction of discounted market trading. When I reported for training in early 1996, the worm had turned. All the major brokerage houses were chasing Merrill Lynch's strategy shift and beginning to flip from transactional platforms to advisory platforms. It was a bit confusing learning how to cold call prospects in the morning and being schooled on estate planning, asset management, and how to develop a brand as an advisor. The title "stockbroker" disappeared across the industry in 1996, replaced with Financial Advisor or Investment Advisor.

It took the industry a few years to change its value delivery systems and brand image completely, and restructure internally by acquiring institutional asset management and analytics firms. They shifted traditional emphasis from sales techniques and sales goals to asset collection and holistic value creation for the client. They also changed the way they selected new talent.

Advisors in this new age had to be older, wiser, interesting, and smart. They had to be strategic planners and thoughtful influencers. They had to be able to make the high-net-worth client comfortable with the big picture. Yes, things were certainly changing and changing fast. I wasn't involved in any of this strategic change, other than to experience it and eventually see the logic of the shift.

Charles Schwab, Scott Trade, and many other discount trading companies popped up every month, fueled by the simultaneous expansion in capabilities, speed, and security of the rapidly expanding Internet environment. In hindsight, failure to make the tectonic shift from transactional to advisory in the late 1990s might have dealt the old brokerage industry a death blow.

Refining as You Go

Leading strategic change is like tending a garden. You start with a plan, resources, and timing. Then it's you and the veggies against the world. Once the vision is codified, stratified, sanctified, and ready to be implemented, the world decides to participate, too.

There is no such thing as a perfect plan; and even if there was, there is no such thing as perfect execution. Execution is imperfect because we are imperfect, and the universe is determined to humble us, one way or another. So how do we ensure the garden survives long enough to yield a bounty? We achieve this by tending the garden.

Every day, every week, and continuously, until the goal is met, or the strategy is rendered moot by another unforeseen threat or opportunity significant enough to make us pause, regroup, and shift again. This allows the leader ample opportunities to spot and address both progress and roadblocks along the way.

In the SEAL teams we used the concept of taking baby steps in training complex and high-value skills because we knew every individual represented a unique collection of challenges. It took more time and attention—focusing on individuals always does—but it was worth the effort and highly effective, in practice. I suggest you take the same approach to tending the strategy.

Approach your implementation plan from the start by breaking the timeline and major milestones into smaller and smaller mini-plans. These mini-plans are your "baby steps." They are not only achievable in the short run, but also provide you with a way to celebrate progress.

Can you imagine waiting until you stood at the top of Mount Everest before you acknowledged success? I think not. Veteran climbers plan out their ascent, breaking it up into stages and key challenges within stages. In this way, they celebrate dozens of small victories en route to the summit.

Tweak, refine, smooth out, tidy up. Whatever you do, do it consistently. Your attention will be noticed; and unless you are interfering with execution, your attention will be appreciated. I've noticed that my physical presence can have a tremendous positive or negative effect on my team.

If I stay out of the work and simply engage at a personal level, I get credit for caring and for respecting their time and professionalism. However, if I were to descend from my leadership perch and interfere, causing disruption and distraction, I would be perceived very differently. How do you tend to the project without getting in the way? It's easy. Don't play fixer in real time.

Observe, remember, and then take your observations and insights somewhere else to record and reflect upon. Then deliver your thoughts to the team leaders. Let them consider the point raised and either refute them with logic and examples or allow them to have the aha moment of understanding.

Let them take time to solve the issue and come back to you with how they fix the problem. Then they own the insight, the analysis, and the solution. Again, this takes more time than seeing, pointing, and telling; but you must empower the team leads to take responsibility. If you don't, they will assume you have taken on that responsibility, absolving them of accountability.

Budget Mismanagement Can Kill the Dream

Unless your company is owned by a multibillionaire who doesn't care how much you spend, you will be held accountable to a budget. The strategic project should be managed well and be accountable to the sources of funding who greenlit your vision. Budgets are boring and inhibit creativity, but budgets keep businesses grounded. If you do your original homework well, you will begin your audacious journey with a smart and achievable budget.

This tool should be frequently monitored and measured to ensure you see positive and negative spending trends early and often. A project of this nature, strategic change, can take many months and even years to complete. Don't allow the duration of the effort lure you into a false sense of financial security.

Checking the budget every quarter won't work. If you do that, the powers that be will see your problem before you do. Anticipate, squirrel away unspent resources when you're ahead, and use this surplus to level out periods when you are forced to spend more than projected. I encourage my leaders to establish a rational and achievable budget, then adjust to account for project streamlining and efficiency to improve over time.

I assume this is possible because the baby steps approach to project management also allows the leaders and team members multiple opportunities to save money through innovative thinking and creativity. The surprises should originate from outside the company.

If the economy or the market is altered significantly from your original thesis, then it may be time to pause and reconsider the entire game plan to ensure the vision is still attainable and justified. For example, say your company is working hard to tap into a government-sponsored, massive national infrastructure building program. You anticipated this and convinced your company to change their strategy to align with this incredible opportunity.

Everything is on track a year into your strategic initiative when a new Congress rolls in and severely reduces or squashes the program altogether. Another version of this story might reflect a situation where a moderate infrastructure program you are preparing for is super-sized by an incoming Congress. You can control the internal aspects of the project, but external events and trends you relied on to make your strategic case might abandon you midstream. Be prepared to take corrective action.

Cost overruns happen in business. In the filmmaking industry, running over budget for too long risks the project being cancelled. Construction projects are also vulnerable to overspending, often resulting in the bankruptcy of the construction company. I've beat the drum on the difference between visionary thinkers, leaders, and everyone else. It is a thing.

Don't forget that the bean counters and average leaders, who saw risk in every PowerPoint slide you briefed, are waiting to take your idea down. They didn't approve in the beginning, and they are lying in wait, hoping to be proven right. You can confirm their bias by mismanaging the assets pledged to the strategic initiative.

You can win the concept battle and lose the execution fight by not managing the project budget to the penny. The world is full of great ideas poorly executed; don't add your baby to that long list of failures. Stay the course, manage well, and don't give the naysayers a chance to shut you down.

Inspiring the External Stakeholders

I often wonder how many times Moses had to rally the Israelites during the forty-year journey to the Promised Land. I'm pretty sure he didn't give them one good pitch in Egypt and then start walking, assuming his message would sustain everyone for the duration of the trip. While I'm no Moses, I do realize a team making a journey of many months, or maybe years, requires steady leadership and a sustained program of inspiration.

You should always be answering the unspoken question, "Why?" Why this strategic direction? Why spend precious resources on this idea? The outside stakeholders and decision makers also are asking this question about your visionary quest. Perhaps nobody asks out loud; but if left unanswered, these questions will evolve into complaints, poor morale, and at the higher level of play, formal agenda items.

Make the rounds. If necessary, write down a "touch" schedule. List the team leaders and the team members. Then list your boss or your bosses, the senior money folks, your board, anyone who has a stake in your success and would intervene if you are failing. Create a contact plan and don't stop communicating to all these constituents until the day the project is successfully completed.

Always adhere to the theory that good news can wait, but bad news must be delivered by a responsible leader as soon as it is received. This track record calms everybody down, inhibiting flights of fantasy regarding your progress or lack thereof. Be consistent with bad news; and if possible, place it in context.

If you anticipated the possibility and have contingencies established to deal with it, say so. Don't delay the telling to gain time for emergency planning. Don't ever let someone else deliver the bad news because you need to stall. Bite the bullet, step up, and say the words. Then go solve the challenge. Keep everyone involved, and just as important, keep everyone inspired!

Chapter Fourteen

Failure, Disappointment, and Resets

Many of life's failures are people who did not realize how close they were to success when they gave up.
Thomas Edison

Navy SEAL training is a series of failures, exquisitely constructed dilemmas, traps, and puzzles designed to confound and disappoint. By the time a SEAL has been through the process of learning this way for a few years, he is immune to the doubt, self-criticism, and negative effects of failure on motivation. However, for those first few years, it is a struggle to believe in yourself wholeheartedly, to be sure of your execution, regardless of what they throw at you.

When I was a teenager starting my SEAL journey, I had no aspirations to be a business leader. After leaving the military, it took me five years to see the value of my SEAL training applied to running businesses. It's more than not quitting. That is the shallow takeaway associated with surviving special operations selection and the intense training that follows. No, it goes deeper, much deeper.

The good news for you is this is a learned skill. Anyone can become resilient, tough, and motivated in the worst of situations. To be a successful visionary leader, you must address failure and your response to failure head-on. Understanding yourself so you can begin to correct your response to stress and failure through awareness and, yes, training.

Failure Equals Opportunity

I have a saying that reflects my personal philosophy regarding failure. It's a mantra of sorts that's easy to follow and easy to pass on with confidence, because I have personally failed so many times, yet survived to fight and win again. This philosophy is simple: failure equals opportunity. I fail, I take stock of my failure, I assess what I need to do differently or better, and then I move forward.

Another way to think of this is to say the word *opportunity* in your mind every time you fail. This is an exercise you should perform all the time, not just at work. Practice this, and it becomes behavior over time. I wrecked my car; what can I learn from that? My spouse is angry because I messed up; how can I pull a lesson from that to evolve?

Life is a coin with one side marked *failure* and the other *opportunity*. Study any self-made millionaires and billionaires, and you'll find lots and lots of failures. Yet these people stood up, dusted off, and became smarter, tougher, and more successful. You can do it, too!

Pilot FAA Certification

I've wanted to be a pilot since I was a teenager. When I was in my twenties, I ordered the study course for ground school so I could take the FAA exam. I didn't know how I was going to pay for the actual flying lessons, but at least I could learn about flying while traveling all over the world in the SEALs. This dream didn't come true, at least not when I was young.

In 2010, I began flight lessons and ground school study anew. I loved the experience and was able to remember the information sufficiently to qualify for the FAA examiner to test my skills and knowledge. I breezed through the oral exam, then took off, the examiner in the seat to my right. I performed every task to perfection and was feeling very pleased with myself when he asked me to do something I didn't understand. I really didn't remember the answer or the procedure he referred to. I was so close, but the examiner failed me.

I didn't have to retake the oral exam; and a few weeks later, I passed the flying portion of the private pilot requirement.

The thing is, I'd never failed an academic test. I was a great student and had never failed to pass any proficiency test I'd trained for in my life. Never. Even after I passed the second time, I was bothered by this uncharacteristic event. I eventually shrugged it off and began to fly regularly.

A year or so later, I decided to become an instrument-rated pilot. This is the same set of skills and knowledge professional airline pilots must learn to be certified to fly passenger planes. It took me longer to prepare; but when test day came, I was ready. I aced the three-hour oral exam and couldn't wait to get into the cockpit. Then it happened. I was going to be evaluated by the same FAA examiner.

He was professional, but it started to mess with my head. After successfully completing ninety percent of the flying test, I screwed up. He failed me again. I was retrained and passed a month later, but the lessons I learned were humbling. I decided to accept that failure, even academic and performance failure, was a part of life if you continued to challenge your boundaries. Now, I look back at those two tests and laugh. Failure made me stronger.

Failure to Anticipate

I remember studying the history of warfare through the ages as a young SEAL officer, and in one book the author presented a list of reasons why military commanders fail. At the top of the list, and emphasized as the most prevalent reason, was failure to anticipate. This form of leadership failure can occur at all three levels of business: tactical, operational, and strategic.

Military strategic failures can be reviewed and evaluated, because they were public and often epic in proportion. Private business failures are not so easy to observe and study; yet they happen every day, all around us. Perhaps you've been a part of one or two, as I have.

My experience, thankfully, is in watching my senior leaders suffer strategic shortsightedness and, yes, failure to anticipate. Being a visionary leader, a true diviner of the future, should inoculate you somewhat from this risk; but it still can happen. Napoleon failed to anticipate the vast geography of Russia and the brutal winters when he destroyed his grand army in a vain attempt to conquer that nation.

My latest failure to anticipate was all about failure to anticipate parabolic success. I failed to think it might happen and, in my case, I was being counseled to be more pedestrian in my outlook by my funding partners. Alas, we were all wrong. I was wrong to scale back our vision of growth and opportunity, and they were wrong to apply standard caution and conservative brakes on the collective dream.

The result was crazy growth and running short on resources. We stuttered and sputtered for a year, slowing the growth artificially to catch our wind, then we were off to the races again. I learned my lesson. Never second-guess a good strategy, well-contrived and well-executed. Stand tall and push back on the naysayers, the foot draggers, and "seasoned" technical experts, who want things to be ordered and incremental. Sometimes pursuing your vision is anything but organized and predictable. Anticipate everything in your planning, even success, especially success!

Failure to Act

There are plenty of examples in history that demonstrate what happens when leaders fail to act. A combination of failure to act can be found when we examine the American Civil War, specifically the Battle of Gettysburg. The Army of Northern Virginia, under the command of General Robert E. Lee, executed a strategic movement into Pennsylvania. An invasion of the north designed to attrite the Union Army and strike fear in the minds of northern politicians sitting in Washington, DC. If successful, Lee believed this fear would result in peace negotiations and an end to the bloody conflict.

General Lee was a master of maneuver warfare and was known to pick his fights with great care and planning. He separated his forces to approach Pennsylvania in several lines of march, sending his cavalry far and wide to find the union army and to sow rumors of a great rebel invasion. As always, Lee expected to select his battleground with care and lure the north into a decisive engagement.

As the Union Army of the Potomac, under General George Meade, cautiously moved west, advance elements of General Lee's forces stumbled into a fight with Union Calvary near the town of Gettysburg, Pennsylvania. Before Lee could stop it, his leaders at the front of the march began to commit, decisively engaging the Union Cavalry to crush the small force.

Lee rushed to the sound of a raging battle, and upon arrival, he realized he was on the wrong ground to influence a decisive victory. Even worse, the union forces held the high ground and were steadily being reinforced. Lee had precious few hours to decide to disengage. He considered the ground and the growing enemy forces facing him and decided to stay and fight.

Military scholars opine that Lee could have and should have withdrawn his forces early in the engagement to seek a fight elsewhere, on his terms. One of his top generals noted in his published memoirs years after the war that the general staff argued with Lee on this very point. Detractors in the North claimed Lee suffered from hubris and vanity, while some in the South hinted Lee wasn't healthy, a failing heart impacting his judgment.

We'll never know why Lee stayed to fight. But we do know he lost the battle, and as a result the strategic push into the north was also a failure. The rebels would never again threaten the North on their own ground. Lee's failure to act—despite realizing the position of his army was untenable and contrary to the strategic purpose of the invasion—is an example of a seasoned leader letting momentum, and perhaps pride, influence his judgment.

In the 1990s, the SEAL community was focused on hard-hitting, direct-action mission sets. Missions that emphasized speed, shock, and extreme tactical execution on target. This was almost the opposite of the SEALs methodology in Vietnam, where stealth, guile, and patience were the keys to special operations success. It became apparent that by the 1990s, our senior enlisted leaders were all new-generation (post-Vietnam) veterans trained in the new missions, almost to the exclusion of anything else.

This was affecting the way our young officers were being raised as decision makers. Our leaders were committed to victory on the ground, at any cost. SEALs were learning how to charge machine-gun nests. This concerning trend was identified and corrected by instituting clever training scenarios into all SEAL training exercises and my retooling the leadership training received by our junior officers.

The clever scenarios baited officers into attacking a target that was clearly not what they expected. Two guards on site in the intelligence briefing became twenty on site. Many officers attacked anyway, even though outgunned and outnumbered. Sometimes the action required is for a leader to walk away.

Failure to Accept

It bears noting again that accepting information that is contrary to tradition, your philosophy, or the plan, is difficult for most leaders. We all get entrenched, dialed in, and focused. It's what leaders do, day in and day out. Tenacity is a valuable attribute for a leader, but what happens when the unthinkable occurs? Your visionary plan may not survive contact with reality.

This could happen for many reasons. How will you react to this turn of events? Failing to accept reality is a consequence of avoidance behavior we are all susceptible to experiencing. So it's okay to pout, but only for a few minutes. Then it's time to rethink the possible. As we've learned studying black swan events, these events are difficult and often life-changing; but the reaction of leaders to the events are prone to making a bad situation much worse.

How long should you wait before accepting the reality in front of you? Is five minutes acceptable? What about an hour? There are no set rules for this, and you shouldn't look for any. My advice is for you to gauge the impact of the event or new information on your plan by assessing how long it will take to rework things and regain momentum.

You need to make an initial, almost intuitive assessment. Create a new timeline for action, then pull your team together to get more minds working the problem. If the plan is moot, restart the vision quest process with a dream team, followed by the critical analysis team. Reboot, rethink, recreate, and start executing again, as soon as possible. To do anything else invites drift, paralysis, or true strategic failure.

I run into this from time to time when key talent decides to leave unexpectedly. Everybody, me included, stares at their desk when this happens. Going thorough recent history to remember if there any hints. Did we push them away? Why didn't they give us an opportunity to counter? The longer we muse and delay action, the longer it takes to solve the staffing shortfall challenge. Should we find a temp or consultant to fill in? How about using an agency to find the long-term answer?

The correct leader response is the same for this situation as it is for larger projects or strategic change initiatives. It is what it is. Face it, act, stop second-guessing, stop running the past through your mind like an old movie. Take the hit, accept it, and move forward. Always move forward!

Failure to Adapt and Evolve

So, let's say something happened that knocked your strategic project off the rails. You've anticipated that things like this might happen; and when it did, you took it in stride, not wasting any time on regrets or recriminations. You and your team are poised to act, and everyone is enthusiastic. What's a leader to do? I suggest your first actions should be to challenge every element of the plan left to execute.

Resource access and cost, timing and timelines for key milestones, talent readiness, retention, and competency. Think of how you might act after a car accident. You assess your health, the passenger's health, then get out and survey the car by doing a three-hundred-and-sixty-degree inspection.

You were on your way to grandma's house, and that's five hundred miles away. No worries, you have AAA accident towing coverage and a rental car on your insurance policy, both put in place a year ago for just this contingency. Sure, it sucks to have your car smashed up, but in this case your leadership has ensured the family can still get to grandma's house for the weekend. Mission accomplished.

It wouldn't make sense to sit on the side of the road and go through the accident or to start making repairs on the car. Leaders know bad things happens, setbacks occur, and they prepare themselves and their teams psychologically and mechanically by being ready for the unexpected.

Another behavior observed in effective leaders is the ability to adapt to the situation. In the SEALs, this was a key quality expected in a combat leader. The assumptions baked into the plan fade like smoke by the time the team sees the target for the first time. The two bad guys you were told to expect are now twenty and the moderate weather report briefing you received is wrong; in fact, there's an inbound storm front.

We were taught to accept the conditions as we found them, and then act by adapting to that new reality. You can practice this (and train your team as well) by leveraging each change event that affects your progress. Use the opportunity to evolve professionally, think, resolve, and work the problem.

While chaos and turmoil are usually messy, they do provide

opportunities to excel. For example, let's say an unforeseen event or piece of information affects your entire industry.

There's an old saying: "He who hesitates is lost." In the world of business competition, you could say the company that hesitates is also lost. Anticipating, accepting, adapting, and evolving give the enlightened leader and his or her team a decisive competitive advantage.

This mindset and leadership methodology takes the worst of situations and converts the chaos into gold. Often, the visionary outcome is unaffected. It is the plan of how to reach that visionary point on the horizon that must be retooled. I learned this lesson the hard way, in the SEAL teams, and as an investment professional.

Channeling Emotional Energy

It might sound like I'm asking you to be a robot, free of emotions. That couldn't be further from the truth. Great leaders are sensitive to social energy, empathetic to individual crises, and emotionally attached to the people they lead and serve. Their job may not allow for demonstration of emotion, at least not emotions that might spook the team, convey despair, or exhibit displaced anger.

An effective leader controls these negative impulses, even while feeling them surge inside. An inspirational leader must face a threat head-on and then channel the power of his or her emotions into action. Nothing I've experienced in two decades in business has come close to the loss of life in combat. But even in that scenario, a good leader pulls the team together, reminding them they are not immortal, but they do have a noble purpose. They have the team, and they have the man standing on either side, brothers who rely on every teammate to be switched-on, vigilant, and professional. There's always time to mourn once the fight's been won.

Resilient leaders have a good sense of humor. How else can

they survive all the trials and tribulations of being accountable? Humor is also a positive outlet for emotional pressure. Failure breeds disappointment, and disappointment fosters defeatism. SEALs feel it, movie stars feel it, top politicians feel it, and you will feel it, too. It's what you do with that disappointment that makes all the difference.

If you have a hard time seeing the humor in disaster, try a simple smile instead. I've been freezing cold, shivering beyond control, my mind focused on my misery, only to have a shift change of mindset when I saw another victim in my team smiling at me. It humbled me and made me realize I wasn't as tough as I thought, definitely not movie hero tough.

I don't think the cliché, rah-rah speech rallies professionals the way it does high school athletes, so I don't recommend this approach. Instead, make your firm confidence known, one person at a time, by walking among your team and asking how they are doing. Courage is contagious. Your demeanor will set the tone and show the team all is not lost. There's no need for fancy words, just simple human contact. Project strength and purpose, and then act!

Some of the most courageous and inspiring SEAL leaders I knew were so soft-spoken we had to lean in to hear what they were saying. This is a practiced art, so practice at home as well as at work. Be resolute, but not stiff and inhuman. Be empathetic, but firmly push forward and through the mess to the other side. Have a sense of humor. Life goes on, and it's more enjoyable with a smile on your face!

Clear-Minded Reset

We've arrived! You have a handle on the crazy, and you've started the reassessment process. You've projected calm and met with all the key players to make sure they know you are going to make it all work. A reset is required if most of the visionary plan is disrupted or destroyed by the intervening event. Don't push the old plan forward and hope for the best. Disengage, reassess, and start making a new plan.

On several occasions in and out of the military, I've found myself going all the way back to square one. It feels wrong, like a tweak or adjustment to the plan should be enough. But in certain circumstances, it is not enough. Depending on the criticality of the strategic outcome, you can start from scratch and accelerate the new plan, working nights and weekends to make up for all the lost time spent on the first iteration of the plan.

The team you lead should hear this from you. You need to lay out the path to a total reset and ask for a full commitment to get back on the original timeline. It's time for you to repeat the visionary purpose of the exercise, how the team will impact the course of your company's history strategically.

Infuse them with positive energy, reignite the quest, and convert them into true believers all over again. Then ask them to do the impossible. I've taken men all night through terrible terrain, only to realize the only way to meet the target timeline is to retrace my steps to the beginning of the journey and begin again, with a quarter of the time remaining to execute.

In times like these, leaders earn their pay. Managers can monitor normal; leaders are required to drive excellence, especially when the universe is bound and determined to divert, delay, and defeat their efforts. Clear your mind and set the new course. Full steam ahead!

Chapter Fifteen

Turning the Corner

The woods are lovely, dark and deep. But I have promises to keep, And miles to go before I sleep, And miles to go before I sleep.
Robert Frost

SEAL tactical instructors have a game they play that serves to teach an important lesson. That lesson is simple yet poignant: it's never over until it's over. SEAL training in resilience, mental and physical, starts with basic screening and training at the Special Warfare Training Center in Coronado, California, and doesn't end until the day you take the uniform off for the last time.

The instructors push the trainee's endurance envelope and create tactical puzzles that allow the SEAL leaders and their men time to make the decisions that result in success or an extended period of pain and misery. I can still remember the first time I stood on the edge of the woods in northern Virginia, freezing, on the brink of hypothermia after four days' movement over difficult terrain in the cold and driving rain.

We were not issued clothing to protect us; and to make matters worse, we were each carrying one hundred pounds of gear on our backs. So I was ecstatic when I heard the whomp, whomp sound of the helicopter moving closer in the night, heading right for our position.

Three of us were holding infrared lights forming a triangle, the signal that it was a safe landing zone. I was kneeling at the top of the triangle, face and light angled up. I couldn't wait to get warm and eat real food again. Then it happened. The helicopter paused above us for thirty seconds as if confused. I wanted to yell, to gain their attention. Didn't they see the lights? They had to see the lights.

Then, like in the movies, the helicopter spun slowly on its axis and began to leave. I was stunned. We were all stunned. The aircraft left, and we waited another ten minutes. Surely they wouldn't fly all that way and not pick us up; that wasn't rational. Yet that is exactly what happened. Our leader pulled us closer and reminded us there was a briefed protocol if we missed our pickup. He made the radio call, and we waited for the results. It wasn't a good message. We'd been given another pickup point and time, two days patrol farther into the rugged Virginia landscape.

I lived this emotional experience over and over in the SEAL teams until the lessons were burned into my character. I learned to push through any task until it was truly completed. Success was the only end worth reaching. As I became more experienced, I watched new guys live through the feelings of abandonment, rage, and disappointment as the training instructors changed the rules again and again.

I also watched them grow stronger, more confident, and more resilient. A select few were already immune to promises, but many of us had to learn to ignore the emotions and logical voices in our heads and focus on executing the job at hand. Resilience is a learned trait. In business, enlightened leaders may teach it to their teams and employees. But more often it is learned much the same way I learned it: broken promises, illogical disruptions, a loss of funding, or an unexpected change of plans.

At this point in your visionary journey, you are getting close to the prize. The idea was sound, your plan was spot on. You've had to adjust, alter, or reset along the way; but now you are close, so close you can hear the helicopters coming.

It's Not Over Until It's Over

There's a sense of accomplishment, of validation, when the strategy begins to make obvious sense to everyone else. It may take weeks, months, or even years to happen; but when it does happen, there's no feeling quite like it for a visionary leader.

There's a saying in the SEAL teams that is useful for keeping your feet on the ground and your eyes on the prize. "It's not over until it's over."

When you feel the turn, when it is clear the plan is taking shape and everything anticipated and prepared for is in sync with the timeline, that's when you need to start paying attention to motivational drift. Your leaders, you, the team are all human; so it's easy to understand that the closer you get to the goal, the easier it is to slack off a bit. To coast. This is a period fraught with risk, for the assumption of success is not success.

There are countless sports videos showing runners, car drivers, and football players slowing down just as they approach the end of the race or the goal line, only to be passed at the last second, to be tackled or stripped of the ball only yards from making a touchdown. Apathy from a false sense of achievement is a real thing, for normal people and even elite teams.

Pay attention to the work ethic, the drive to solve problems in real time vs waiting until next week. These are all indicators that the smell of success in the wind is impacting motivation. You are the leader of this strategic enterprise; so when you see these signs, step in and lead. First make sure your subordinate leaders stay switched on; then together as a leadership team, focus on the rest of the group. Steady pressure, watch the clock, get the vison across the finish line, then relax and celebrate. Not a minute sooner.

Military history, especially infantry history, is replete with examples of why staying on guard until you are safely home is important. Patrols leaving a base are always alert, awake, and attentive to the terrain, the threat environment, and the rest of their unit and assigned leaders. In Vietnam, in Iraq, and in Afghanistan, there are many stories told by special operators, Marines, and Army soldiers, who relaxed their posture the closer they came to their base of operations.

The enemy knows this, too, so they set up ambushes and

other little surprises on the routes to the bases, hoping to catch the once-vigilant fighters off guard. Don't let this happen to you. When you see you are turning the corner on the downward slope of the strategic project, sharpen up. Become more alert, not less. Remember, it's not over until it's over!

Frustration Management

In my post-military experience, I've failed to act in one significant leadership category numerous times: removing a poor or ineffective leader. I began my adulthood in the military, where a leader was expected to work with his team, to improve them over time. There was no human resources department, and no layoffs, reductions in force, or terminations.

As a result, after I was out of the military, I found out I was an enabler. I would train, mentor, and coach employees and leaders and hope for a turnaround. In many cases this didn't happen, and the organization suffered as a result. I know this is my Achilles' heel, and I'm mindful of this trait now; but there was a time early in my civilian life when my biggest failures fell into this distinct category.

Leading dynamic change is difficult. It takes energy to be positive all the time. To cheer people on when you've had a bad day. To keep focused on the horizon and the all-important end goal. That's why you need to police yourself and your leaders to ensure they don't succumb to frustration, irritability, and don't become hypercritical of the project and the team.

Frustration is human, and there will always be reasons, legitimate ones, for people to see the world as a glass half-empty. When frustration becomes caustic, when it negatively affects morale and even execution, that's when you must act and act quickly. The period after the turning point in a project and before final success has less fear of failure, less uncertainty.

This also means a team may begin to lose their grip on why the project and their contribution is vital to the company's survival or success. People bond together and to their leaders in times of doubt and stress and relax that commitment as the threat or opportunity becomes less and less of a challenge. You can't be everywhere or do everything, but you can watch for the few people who would knowingly or unknowingly pull your team apart.

Don't enable this behavior to either keep a leader in place or to keep the team together. Address it and fix it, or deal with it by replacing the negative element. Nothing personal; everybody must pull together, all the time, all the way. You cannot achieve visionary change with mediocre efforts.

Change requires courage in everybody, not just the leadership; so make sure everyone is tracking and motivated. If someone isn't pulling their weight, try to speak with them, but don't enable the behavior. There are likely other projects or tasks they are suited to perform elsewhere, so cut them loose and fill the empty spot on the bench with a happy, energetic person. Trust me—waiting too long can allow the bad attitudes to become contagious.

Focus, Focus, Focus

Another way to avoid mission fatigue or pull back as you approach the end of your journey is to double down on the little things. People who are distracted, content, or bored tend to disregard or ignore the fine points first. Establish a discipline for measuring and reporting execution of tasks in finite detail. This is where you will detect the first wobbles, the first signs of drift. Professionals want to perform well. First for themselves, and then for their peers.

These two sources of drive are usually more powerful than working hard to make the leader happy. Don't use negative motivation to tap into these feelings by singling out the slackers. Instead, celebrate the team members who are meeting or exceeding expectations. Work to lift up the C-level performers rather than beat them down.

There's a favorite exercise in SEAL basic training to test a student's commitment to the team. The instructors select a student from the class and have them hold their arms out to their side and parallel to the beach. Then they place a three-pound wood paddle in each hand, each paddle held perpendicular to the beach.

The instructions are simple: if the arms drop enough that the lower end of the paddle touches the student's pants, the class gets punished. The student is told he will not have to join the class if he fails and they get punished due to his weakness. The instructors suggest there is a record time to beat, and the class begins to shout encouragement; but there is no record and there's no time limit either. Eventually the student succumbs to fatigue (usually in less than four minutes) and the paddles slowly come down.

The interesting part of this exercise is about watching the student and watching the class separately. This exercise can be random or used to assess a specific student's mindset. If the student cares about the class, he will struggle valiantly for close to four minutes before slowly failing. Fakers will put on a show of struggling for around two minutes and play it up before failing dramatically, quickly lowering the paddles.

In the case of the first type of student, they almost always refuse the pardon and join their class for the punishment. However, the second type of student rarely does. Picture the second student warming themselves by the fire while the class is rolling around in the freezing ocean water. An instructor will calmly point out the obvious focus on self rather than team, and in many cases the second type of student will realize the mistake they made and run to join their class. Sadly, most do not, even after gentle mentoring.

By the way, please do not set up exercises of this sort in your company. I share this with you to show that even in elite, volunteer organizations, tough times define character and behavior. Maybe a member of the team wanders away rather than pitching in. Or someone works a nine to five schedule while the rest of the team is working nine to ten hours a day until a critical task is completed. Focus on the little things and on the behaviors. If you do, you'll have advance warning and plenty of time to intervene in a positive way.

Head Count

In small elite units, there is a patrol process called taking a head count. This isn't about votes—it's a way for the leader and the team to confirm that everybody is okay and still with the patrol. This is conducted whenever a patrol leaves a safe place, passes through an unsafe place, halts temporarily, and completes the mission.

If a team is being extracted by a vehicle, such as a boat or helicopter, the leader is the last to board. This is because the leader is counting heads as each patrol member enters the extraction platform. Taking a head count is a good way to gauge if your visionary team is still with you. Physically, of course; but more importantly, mentally.

The tasks handed to high-performance teams are stressful by nature. While you try to select people capable of executing the job, you also need to be mindful of the psychological makeup of the individuals that make up the team. I go into this process of talent alignment in great depth in my first book, *Be Nimble,* because it is a critical foundation for team and leader success.

Many technically astute and gifted employees melt under any kind of pressure. Others can handle pressure, but can only work alone, project teamwork irritates them. Then there's the speed of accurate work.

I've been using speed as a metaphor for many years. It goes something like this: There are two kinds of professionals. Those who move at a fifty-miles-an-hour speed and those capable and happy to move at one hundred miles an hour.

If your organization or team is set on a task that requires one-hundred-miles-an-hour level of effort and mental focus, then don't staff it with fifty-miles-an-hour people. If you do, then you'll leave those people behind. They will be frustrated and unhappy and so will their one-hundred-miles-an-hour teammates.

In my experience, this is a team design flaw that can be avoided at the beginning of the journey. It's also my experience that even a great leader will be challenged, or fail, when trying to convert a slow-speed employee into a high-speed employee. As a side note, a slow, methodical research project should be staffed with the slower and more methodical employee. A high-speed employee will be miserable in this paradigm. As with a foot patrol, you are only as fast as your slowest SEAL. Take head counts frequently.

Rally the Troops—Bring It Home

It's customary to celebrate the conclusion of a project. An emotional ending to an emotional trek. In keeping with a renewed focus on the little things after turning the corner, I suggest you find interesting ways to celebrate the small victories as well. Especially as you get closer to the prize.

I've been beating the complacency and apathy drum here not to warn you of what might happen, but to warn you about what will happen. People need to know they are a team and that the team is in it to win it, whatever it is. When pushing a visionary project, it's important to remember that your team will be targeted continuously by the employees on the outside looking in.

Fear of change will not disappear until the change is locked in and becomes the new normal. This means your strategic project team could be perceived as a force arranged and focused on destroying the status quo. The same status quo the rest of the organization would like to preserve.

So put your team on a pedestal and celebrate the little wins. Push them harder than status quo workers push themselves, and then reward them for it. Use surprises like midday parties, unannounced compensation time off, guest lecturers, or even comedians. I'm not encouraging you to create a drinking band of pirates. I'm just saying happy is as happy does.

Allow time to be happy and relaxed. Working hard all the time may be tolerable for high-speed teams, but everyone needs a break now and again—even leaders, even you. For most high achievers, a timely distraction in the team's work environment will not be debilitating, only enjoyable.

In our headquarters office, we have two Jenga puzzles, a corn hole game, and a ring/hook game. Anyone can engage in playing these games anytime it suits them. When everyone trusts the work ethic and professional integrity of their teammates, including their leaders, a break from the grind doesn't raise eyebrows.

Schedule the motivational events, rewards, and breaks as you would a task. Make it a part of your leadership responsibility to ensure that the pace of happiness is maintained, right across the finish line. I've been part of nearly one hundred bid and proposal teams. Efforts that had us working crazy hours every day for weeks and even weekends. I can't remember one that incorporated this idea of continuous celebration. In fact, as each project element was completed on the way to submission, the teammates simply peeled off and disappeared.

As a rule, the only people left standing on the last day of the proposal project were the editors and folks charged with boxing up, or electronically transmitting the proposal for delivery. Don't forget the rally for the last leg of the project. Raise morale, sustain the team bond, then finish strong and together!

Finish Strong

Competitive athletes and elite organizations focus on changing the world. They train, plan, and sacrifice to make their mark;

and once they've succeeded, they move the target farther away, challenging themselves all over again. Extreme sports are famous for this mentality; so are special operations professionals. Their skills and knowledge may be wildly different from yours, but that doesn't mean you cannot emulate their spirit, their drive to conquer their fears and to achieve greatly.

If you are a leader or aspire to be one, then you already have a special commitment to the greater good, the bigger win. Leaders are useless in the blah, steady-as-she-goes world. Managers can handle the humdrum of systems and process oversight. But you, no, you are set on another path altogether!

What have we learned about leading and living through the last few steps on the way to success? Well, we know that people are different, and they react differently to stress, challenges, long hours, and rewards. We know it takes planners and critical thinkers to execute the implementation of a dream. But it takes an engaged leader to shepherd the team from a project's hopeful beginning, through its discordant middle phases, and finally to push or pull the team to a triumphant conclusion.

Don't underestimate the power of a decisive, insightful, and empathic leader. Stay in the fight every step of the way, watch over every disturbance, cheer people on individually and as a group, celebrate the little wins, and always point to the horizon.

You started the journey full of energy and passion; don't fade out over time. You must repeat the mantra of why the work is sacred, valuable, game changing. If faced with a dire threat, don't dwell on the downside implications of the risk. Instead, hammer home how valuable it is to strategically intercept that threat. Communicate how you, the team, the company, will disrupt the danger and turn the situation to your collective advantage.

Don't be passive or defensive; attack the threat and keep the team focused on leaning into the visionary solution that you all believe will neutralize that strategic risk. Lead, be a leader, lead your subordinate leaders, and let your people see and hear you as you communicate all that is required to ensure victory. Hourly, daily, weekly, monthly. Do not be absent; your presence is a clear sign that you care as much as they do about the outcome. Be a visionary beacon for change. Oh yeah and have a little fun while you're doing it!

Chapter Sixteen

Strategic Success

The greatest danger for most of us is not that our aim is too high and we miss it, but that it is too low and we reach it.
Michelangelo

Success at last! You did it! You identified the threat or opportunity, led your dream team to confirm your insights and intuitions about the future, brought in a critical team of focused experts to shape the dream into a project, and then pitched it until approved. No mean feat, I can assure you. So now what?

In my experience, strategic success is less a fixed milestone and more a continuum. That's just the way it is. This continuing evolution may not be dramatic or visionary, but it should still be happening, at least in a healthy and vigorous organization. Stagnation is a disease that destroys value. That goes for companies and people. It is important to bask in the limelight of your success for a while, but then get back to work.

In the last chapter, we discussed attitudes and momentum challenges you might experience when you've turned the corner and are heading for the goal. Another phenomenon that challenges leaders as they near the finish line is what I call the easy slide. The easy slide means to shorten the timeline and create a false end state, an easier target to achieve. Why would anyone do such a thing?

Well, we're all human; and coasting or dumbing down the goal a little is also human. Why not change a few metrics to arrive at "good enough?" When a leader gets close, real close, they may be fatigued after so many weeks or months of pushing, pulling, and prodding the team toward the objective. Superiors, external stakeholders, and resource providers might also be suffering from battle fatigue, encouraging you to declare victory early.

Ending your hard work a bit early guarantees a win, stems the resource burn, and releases the valuable team talent back to other projects and tasks. You may not be tempted to do this, but your benefactors may see things differently. In the beginning, you shaped the vision of what success could be...should be. I say stay the course! See it through to the end of the race, regardless of the temptation to stop short and declare victory. Shake off the temptation to gain a cheap reward and finish what you and your team started.

This is almost always the right thing to do, and it sets an example, creates a precedent for future strategic work. You and your teammates will be known as visionary engineers, builders of a new future. You will also have won the respect of your peers, senior management, and perhaps your industry.

So, I will assume you are the kind of leader who, once your mind is made up, delivers what was promised. Now that you've completed the strategic project, there are a few things you should do before the glow dissipates. The first is to reward your team. Thanking them for their sacrifice and effort is a given, but I mean a real gesture of value. A promotion, a raise, or a cash bonus. A trip or a valuable gift might do.

As a visionary leader, you should achieve victory and never take the team's role in your collective success for granted. I say this having rarely witnessed this done in practice. Usually, the team disperses immediately after crossing the finish line. The successful leader is wined and dined, bonused, and promoted. He or she is often moved immediately to another high-value project and that is that. Don't let this happen.

Document Strategic Processes

Another thing that is worth doing is documenting the project's life span. Preferably during the project, but at least once the project is over. In my experience, visionary projects challenge the status quo in more ways than one. The team ends up creating new processes and procedures, new software, clever workarounds, new operational allies, and new ways of seeing a problem through to a successful conclusion.

This is the flow, the electrical charge a team feels as they accelerate work and thought faster than anyone conceived was possible, smash through limiting assumptions, and innovate or invent their way, one milestone at a time. Lightning in a bottle for sure. Capture all of this if you can. Write it down; document the wins and the losses. Canvass the team after the fact to get their ideas on other radical new improvements in workflow, analysis, or organizing to win.

It is difficult to be mature and dedicated enough to take the time to do all of this, but it is worth it. Trust me. I've watched teams perform, win, then go their separate ways. Whatever they did, whatever they thought, it was lost. The organization didn't see the future value of capturing the magic before it faded. Inevitably, a few years later I'd watch the same challenges being addressed all over again, from scratch. As if nobody had ever solved them in the past.

It was a joke in the Navy that if you survived long enough you could get credit for the same game-changing idea every four to five years. Organizations have short memories because people rely on memory and not archival records of lessons learned. The second failure, if an archive does exist, is ignoring the value stored away for future use.

Training in new methods derived from lessons learned helps. Championing the project histories by converting them to multimedia presentations helps. The culture of winning is fragile and only a few years away from disappearing as people come and go. Capture the magic; spread the word.

Succeeded the Hard Way

When I entered the financial services market, my firm put me through a multi-week orientation course. It was focused mainly on understanding the products, services, and capabilities of the firm to support me as a financial advisor, as I found, closed, and advised high-net-worth individuals or institutions. I found out quickly that most of that course was useless when it came to operating my fledgling practice.

The saving grace was the company's monthly magazine. It touted success stories from all over the company's geographic reach, across all its offerings. I had a few family acquaintances I'd tapped for advice, people with business experience and sales knowledge; but none of these assets were money managers. I decided one day to call the financial advisor showcased in the monthly success magazine. It changed my career.

While none of the lessons learned from our top performers were available institutionally or taught in orientation, the successful players did exist in the flesh. All I had to do was pick up the phone and ask the appropriate product, service, or analysis department in the company one question.

"Can you give me the names of the top two or three financial advisors kicking butt with your product, service, or analytical tool?" Then I would pull up their contact information in the company directory and send an email introducing myself, explaining my lack of knowledge, and requesting a short mentoring phone call. It worked! Nobody turned me down. A few adopted me, keeping up with my progress over the first few years I was in the business.

I owe them all a debt of gratitude for changing my mindset and showing me the shortcuts to winning. I later wondered why the company hadn't done the same thing institutionally. They could have documented the winning formulas and taught them to new blood and the old guard, directly or by having the information readily available and easy to access. It was shortsighted, but typical of the industry at the time. Think about it—you could perpetuate excellence by establishing just such a learning platform or environment. Document your success and pass it on!

Evaluating the Journey

Aside from documenting the success of the project and your team's individual contributions and performance, I believe the end of something epic always calls for honest self-appraisal. My book *Be Nimble* begins with a focus on knowing yourself—your strengths and your weaknesses. How else can we improve? Every successful thing I've accomplished left a trail of missteps, mistakes, failures, and misjudgments behind. I'm acutely aware there is no such thing as perfect performance; therefore, I don't try to attain perfection.

However, I also know that which does not kill me makes me stronger. That is, if I'm honest and candid with myself regarding my leadership. So, after the victory lap and the celebratory dinner, after you've spent the bonus, sit down and take a moment to reflect.

SEALs complete missions and do what's referred to in the military as a hotwash, also called an after-action review or AAR in the US Army. Missions are planned like business projects. There are resources to manage, dollars being spent, labor hours to calculate, and a timeline to follow.

Unlike in business, the definition of success may be weighed and measured in lives saved or lost. SEALs are hypercritical beings. The more experienced they are, the more hypercritical they get. Each man will play the mission over in his head hundreds of times, seeing his role step-by-step in his mind's eye, noting where he executed well and where he did not. Then the screwups and missed opportunities stack up as a new to-do list. Can I fix them on my own before the next mission? Did it help to do so? Who else can I rely on for training and mentoring?

Business leaders should be more like SEALs in this respect. Rather than hope no one saw the mistakes (or if they did, hoping they forget them), a business leader should inventory those failures and attack them with an eye to eliminating the weaknesses before the next critical task or project rolls around.

This doesn't have to be a negative exercise. In fact, I focus only on the shortfalls because I'm confident, post project success, that my strengths outweigh my weaknesses. List the things that went wrong, starting with the initial conception of your visionary insight. If it wasn't yours to begin with, start at the point you became the champion of that vision and its leader. I like to break the self-evaluation into phases from that initial point of reference all the way to the true successful conclusion of the project.

You can certainly conduct incremental, in-process reviews to capture data on execution in near real time. But at a minimum, you should conduct this drill as soon as possible after the project is over. If you were successful, then there is a high likelihood you are being earmarked for another challenge without your knowledge. It shouldn't take more than a day to lay out the phases, cite the issues, and draw up a personal corrective action plan. Fight, win, grow, repeat.

Stay Humble

I harp on this theme throughout this and my first business leadership book, *Be Nimble,* because I believe it is the key to my personal success and that it can be valuable to you, too! Humility isn't lack of confidence, but confidence isn't arrogance either. To be humble is to be open and aware of your surroundings, to be alert to new ideas and new sources of information.

It is human nature to gloat a little, to bask in the limelight after a convincing and long-fought win. Put a few of those wins together, and I assure you it can go to your head, distort your situational awareness, and blunt your sharpest instrument—

your brain. If you take the performance inventory discussed in the last segment, you can hardly be full of yourself. That exercise grounds you as a leader and helps you to rest your humility in preparation for the next big thing.

In practice, it looks like the following: you succeed in bringing home the strategic win. You self-assess, create a list of things to improve on, and start improving. Most winners I know are humble to the point of mild paranoia. They wake up thinking they are falling behind; the last win being the last win, literally. They see competition everywhere, and that competition is gaining on them.

In this mindset, you are a warrior training for the next fight, with no illusion regarding your invincibility. Therefore, it's healthy to evaluate your capabilities and then hone them, improve them, as an ongoing discipline. Be ready to fight by clearing your mind and soaking up fresh insights. Remember, it's rarely the threat you see that gets you; instead, it's the threat you don't see, blinded by your biases and hubris, that takes you down.

Another positive side-effect of establishing and then maintaining your humility is the way it allows you to absorb new data and ideas, cleanly and clearly. Each of us walks around with a lot of psychological baggage. Some good and some not so good. For a leader to be at the top of his or her game, they must be able to empty their mind of this baggage and prepare to learn again, like a child learns.

Children learn by experiencing, seeing, hearing, and remembering. They are rarely judgmental about the information they take in and process. That's because to judge, you need a mental system of comparative analysis; and for that system to work, you need a measurement context to compare things to.

Children eventually will learn and evolve into more advanced-thinking young adults, who struggle to accept diverse and competing concepts and facts. They will be forced to decide, to judge what is true and what is untrue. What is fact and what is fiction. Children are like sponges when they are young. Soaking up information at incredible rates. Being humble helps you think with less judgment. More importantly, it helps you to learn and accept what might be possible, allowing you to think like a child again.

Keep Learning

Learning should be a lifelong discipline for anyone who desires to be successful. I typically read between forty-five and fifty books a year. About one third are related to my profession directly. One third is for pleasure, either novels or topics I have a personal interest in. The final third are the wild card topics. These can be in any category of human activity.

For example, I've recently had an itch to learn more about brain science and the study of athletic flow states. In addition to reading books, I listen to podcasts, stream debates, talks, and speeches, and watch a considerable amount of documentary content on television every week. I break down my time spent engaging with these alternative learning platforms in much the same way, with one third allocated to each of the aforementioned topic areas.

There's no reason why we should stop trying to learn when we finish our formal education. Doing so is, in my opinion, intellectual suicide. Ten years after you finish your graduate degree, an undergrad who's been burning the midnight oil every night learning continuously will pass you by in a flash. Their two to three years is the equivalent of your graduate program, and of course updated and accurate to the new reality.

I take time once again to pound this truth home, only because hubris born of visionary success tends to numb us to our faults. It convinces us, like a top politician is convinced by his handlers, that we are the smartest, the brightest, the best; when in truth we are not.

In ancient Rome, returning generals were granted triumphs after their victories. The entire city would turn out to cheer as the successful general rode through the streets on a gilded chariot, a portion of his army marching behind, as well as wagons filled with plunder. It is written that a servant was tasked with standing behind the general on the chariot, holding a laurel wreath over his head to signify his glory in the eyes of Rome. It is also written that this servant's other task was to whisper into the general's ear the words, "Remember, ye be mortal." A warning that some days you're the hero and other days you might be a zero.

Learning makes it hard to become complacent. The more I see and read and hear, the dumber I feel. You can't help but be humbled if you seek out new knowledge. When I was fifty-one, I decided to get what is the equivalent of a black belt in Muay Thai, also known as Thai Boxing. On my first day, I was told it would take two to three years of commitment. I thought I was disciplined enough to deal with that, so I agreed to the terms and started training.

To put this in context, I was a successful CEO, retired SEAL combat veteran, and in damn good physical condition. While I hadn't been in a fight in twenty-five years, I was confident I had the mindset and the tenacity to do well. Mike Tyson, World Heavyweight Boxing Champion of the world, famously said, "Everyone has a plan until they get punched in the face." That about sums up my reality check on the first day of training.

In the ring, I was just a middle-aged fifty-one-year-old. Nothing special, until I learned how to fight at a much higher level of competency. It took me three years to attain, just as predicted. Never stop learning! Never stop challenging your knowledge and skill! Don't settle for the status quo; accelerate beyond that boundary!

Seeking Your Next Challenge

Depending on how long your visionary project takes to complete, you might find that there's no more strategic worlds to conquer.

Or you may find out that your visionary solution was appropriate and timely, as far as it went; but there's a new wind blowing that threatens to render it all moot. These are just two of the many possibilities you might face when your job is done.

If you're truly a visionary thought leader, then you'll have your ear to the ground the entire time you're actively saving the company. You'll see if your forecasts and projections were spot on, slightly off, or wildly inaccurate. As long as the gist of the original threat or opportunity stays the same, you and your team can and will adjust the plan. But what if the change coming is something new? Something worse? Something better?

Sometimes seeking the next visionary challenge happens while you're working on strategic change already. If this happens, then your company will have to decide. Should they continue apace, supporting your project and goal, or shut that effort down and pivot to face a new situation? It's hard to anticipate these things, but in large corporations there are usually more than enough visionary leaders and assets to deal with more than one issue at a time. However, in smaller companies, this might not be the case. You may find yourself supporting two separate strategic initiatives with fewer assets to support either project.

Prioritization is key, but strategic prioritization is based on an inexact science: seeing the future. If you are in a small to midsize organization and there's a second challenge that rises to the level of strategic concern, offer up your services. At a minimum, you can run the dream team and critical analytics processes to get to a recommendation. Then let someone else lead the least critical of the two projects.

Of course, you might find you've solved the one big strategic issue of the decade and your work is done. What to do? Well, if you love being a visionary thinker, you'll get frustrated quickly focusing on day-to-day operational tasks. I suggest that, before you get too disgruntled, you begin a search for your next strategic role, in another company.

I've had this urge multiple times in my professional life. I solve a big problem and then back to a humdrum existence. I start a new company, it stabilizes, and managers take over. Great threats and opportunities don't pop up on the horizon every day, and certainly not in the same industry or company.

Think about it for a moment. How did it feel to challenge the elites, the traditionalists? How did it feel leading the dream team, taking the concept from incubation to planning to execution? If you feel it's what you should be doing, find a new situation where you are the right leader at the right time, all over again!

What Is Your Endgame?

If you've tracked closely with me through these chapters, you should now feel you have a solid grasp on what it takes to change the world. I don't believe in heroics. I know it legitimately happens, trust me, but even SEALs don't try to be heroes. I believe in leadership. I especially love everything about strategic and visionary leadership. If I can't serve in this capacity where I am now, then I begin scanning the industry for a new landing spot. I also consider becoming a consultant eventually, offering the same insights and leadership guidance, taking on a new project as soon as the old one is completed. That's probably my professional endgame. What's yours?

Are you experiencing a lack of strategic thinking mindset in your company? Are your top leaders paying attention to the future? Do they value leaders who do? They may focus on optimization (companies led by accountants, engineers, and attorneys often do this) as a strategy. Measure, count, assess, set new incremental objectives, and repeat. Steady as she goes. All's good until it's not. Unfortunately, in companies like these, nobody will see the future coming until it runs them over.

Learn optimization methods, software, and planning

techniques so you can apply them to steady-state operating business plans. Optimization is valuable in this context. You may also need this skill set to lead a future visionary project efficiently. Just don't mistake optimization for strategy. If you've learned what you can at this level of play and the senior brain trust is stuck in the mud, run! Run to more intellectually fertile ground.

These organizations do exist. You might have to learn a new industry or become adept in a new sector of the industry you're in now, but don't waste your life or your brain begging fools and cowards to change. It's a losing game. Believe me. I've stayed far too long several times, and only realized later I could have made the move sooner and avoided the angst and the wasted time. Congratulations! We are nearly done with our journey together. Just one more chapter to get you refocused on why being a visionary is so rewarding and so critical, especially in our turbulent and ever-changing times.

Chapter Seventeen

Be Visionary

The visionary starts with a clean sheet of paper, and re-imagines the world.
Malcolm Gladwell

I'm a big fan of the author and thought leader, Malcolm Gladwell. His 2000 book, *The Tipping Point: How the Little Things Can Make a Big Difference,* greatly influenced my business thinking...especially my thinking in the realm of sales and market penetration. Gladwell cited studies by the Center for Disease Control, or CDC, on how viruses gained traction, built momentum, and then grew until reaching a point where the spread went parabolic.

Gladwell deftly applies a series of CDC insights to other categories of life and business, including the spread of ideas. "Going viral" is now a common phrase to describe how an idea, a product, or a person's popularity breaks free from its slow buildup and becomes a phenomenon. I've read and reread the book over the years and purchased multiple copies for my leadership teams at two organizations.

Being a visionary, thinking in big, open-minded terms, is building momentum, and I believe this is due to the shock imposed on all of us by the COVID-19 global pandemic. In fact, the drive to shake off the past and think in a new way is gaining ground, heading for a tipping point. The future, our future, is being reimagined.

My purpose in writing this book began with a single-minded focus on how deep thought, horizonal aptitude, was being squashed by tradition and an over reliance on the use of optimization metrics and software-enabled analytics as a substitute for strategy, for thinking. I outlined *Be Visionary* even as my first book, *Be Nimble,* was beginning a pre-release, eight-month-long marketing phase.

We were in the tenth month of the pandemic, vaccines were distributed for the first time, and there was hope we'd all go back to the old life. We didn't know it at the time, but it wasn't to be. The old ways of doing business and living life had been changed in obvious ways and some not so obvious ways, too. Additional variants and flare-ups in 2021 extended the foundational changes; we were not going back. This, I believe, is not all bad. Historically, great upheavals in society, stimulated by wars, natural disasters, economic collapse, and yes, plagues, also stimulated invention and innovation.

After nearly every modern crash in the US stock market, going back to the late nineteenth century, a new wave of entrepreneurial thinkers dropped out of college, left their safe jobs, and began exercising their minds. Minds now unfettered from the old ways and irrefutable truths. In these disrupted paradigms, opportunities to be different, to make things better, faster, smarter, less expensive, were everywhere.

The Black Death, which raged across Europe from 1347 to 1400, depleted the population dramatically, paving the way for the period known as the Renaissance. The Renaissance was an explosion of human creativity in art, science, engineering, and exploration of new worlds—chief among them, an unknown land that would become America. I feel we may be on the cusp of our own renaissance.

It's been eighty years since the world was last shocked and changed by a cataclysm. World War II was more than just a war in historical terms. It generated a long list of unprecedented inventions and innovations. The entire world order changed and evolved because of four years of devastating disruption. Nuclear power, commercial air travel, new manufacturing techniques, plastics, polymers, and other advances in science and technology were developed across the board.

This isn't a good way to invigorate the world, but it is the predictable outcome of large-scale societal upheavals. As we deal with and eventually tame the pandemic, what can you do to seize upon this unique opportunity? What can you see on the horizon of the possible?

Healthcare Disrupted

I could probably write a book on how to improve healthcare in the United States. As I touched on in prior chapters, in 2015, my business partner and I sold our government services company to our employees, making the company an employee-owned entity known as an ESOP. I stayed on initially for a contracted three years to run the ESOP, but I knew the War on Terror was changing and with it the government's funding of outsourced services.

I convinced my new board of directors to let me acquire a second company, one that was not supporting the government, and therefore diversify our revenue stream and mitigate our operating risk. I began searching for a company to buy, and after a year found a tiny healthcare business serving a niche need in the market. During my year long search, I steadily narrowed my focus every month, discarding one industry at a time until I arrived at healthcare. What I found was crazy.

In 2016, the only new books I found on the healthcare industry were focused on the Affordable Care Act (ACA) or the government mandate to digitize medical records. Neither topic was related to radical improvements in patient care, and being an outsider, I naively assumed the patient was the customer. I was wrong. I stayed confused until I began speaking directly with professionals in the industry; that's when my effort was rewarded with true insight. In healthcare today, the customer isn't right; in fact, the customer isn't a part of the value delivery equation.

The entire industry revolves around how to pay for services, and the customer/patient stands by waiting to be told how to pay. The seller dictates the rules, the way to pay, the services you need, and the scheduling of those services. The healthcare service buyer experience is abysmal, especially when compared to buying processes in other industries. Being a patient is about as pleasant as a trip to the department of motor vehicles.

I saw opportunity to make a positive difference everywhere I looked in 2016; and as I write this, that abundance of opportunity still exists. Healthcare is attracting smart people from other walks of life: from technology, logistics, customer service, hospitality, and other professional skill sets. They become successful early because the bar is set so low in healthcare.

If you focus on the patient experience and quality care, while ignoring the tenured medical experts, you immediately make a mark. This is an accelerating area of opportunity and a place where a visionary leader or entrepreneur can flourish. I've met former construction general contractors killing it in laboratory services, and Silicon Valley venture capital guys streamlining healthcare revenue cycle management by simply using techniques and approaches they used in other industries.

This isn't even innovation; it's transference, like an advanced society contacting a primitive one. See for yourself; you just might find the opportunity of a lifetime to do good work, become wealthy, and save lives, too. Learn to be a master of disruption!

Human Engagement Disrupted

When I was a kid in the 1960s, popular culture promised three things we'd experience in the future. One was a flying car, the second one was the television phone, and the third was the Dick Tracy radio watch. The ability to call someone and see their face was a given in most science fiction movies of the time.

While I'm still waiting for my flying car, we have smart watches, and we got our television phone in 1970 when the first working video phone was demonstrated. It would take another thirty-three years for Skype to be introduced to the masses, and seven more after that for Facetime to be invented. Now, communicating great distances is taken for granted. Still, it took the COVID-19 pandemic to really show us how to communicate and work remotely.

I love the efficiency of remote work. Teleconferencing platforms like Zoom, Microsoft Teams, and Ring Central have made remote work possible for all of us. My interest in communications extends beyond making calls to each other, regardless of format. I also see communications as the process of messaging.

By my way of thinking, all activities that move information content from one person to another are forms of human engagement. How do we send messages to each other and what do these messages consist of? One example of this paradigm shift was also accelerated by the pandemic: the demise of the movie theater.

Innovation is often achieved by combining two dissimilar things that already exist to create an exciting new thing. Innovation in communications was spurred by the invention of untethered, handheld smart phones. These platforms are now a threat to cable companies and to the cinema industry, in that they can pull down and display high-quality content without the need for a physical connection, such as cable service or a physical space to access new content like a movie theater.

When the pandemic shut down cinemas all over the world, it signaled the death of a communications platform. Going to the movies will soon feel like playing music on a record player. Nostalgic, but impractical and incapable of satisfying our never-ending appetite for more content, customized to our personal desires. This isn't over. If you look at communications as content flow, regardless of the content, then you'll see and perhaps benefit from tapping into this significant trend.

Labor Force Disruption

You don't have to be a soothsayer to recognize that the way we work is changing. I've been part of organizations that were hierarchal and others that were loose, like a pirate crew. I've seen hybrids, clusters, teams, and teams of teams. When organizing tasks, I prefer to minimize the number of management layers interacting and observing.

As with many things, form follows function when it comes to work and workflow design, so don't get stuck on any one way to win. With the COVID-19 pandemic, we were all given a pass as leaders to experiment with new ways to get the job done.

Even though the US economy has shifted decisively from manufacturing to services and knowledge-based work, very few companies unilaterally embraced virtual work until the pandemic arrived. Now they don't have much of a choice. Even more startling, many employees don't want to come back to the office.

Managers and leaders face a dilemma. Do they force everyone back into the old work paradigm? Should they order people, who are pulling data and assignments down from the cloud and uploading results to the cloud, to do those tasks from inside a glass and brick box instead of the comfort of their home?

There are certainly jobs that require first, physical proximity to accomplish things; but even these traditional team-based exercises are being done more and more through remote conferencing platforms. This will be evolutionary instead of revolutionary.

Many older members of the workforce enjoy separating their home and work lives. They also enjoy the direct, face-to-face social interaction that can be experienced Monday through Friday in the brick-and-mortar work environment.

Despite the efforts of unions and their political allies, I see the future in the gig/borrow-driven economic approach. Uber, Lyft, Airbnb, Vrbo, and other companies are borrowing underutilized assets and monetizing them through a use share model. In real estate and in executive aviation, lending out your expensive and underutilized asset in exchange for a one-time-use payment, or subscription fee, has been a lucrative and efficient business model for decades.

In the not-too-distant future, we will have flying cars; I believe it in my childish heart. Where will they take off from? Where will they land? How about underutilized rooftops? How many acres of landing pads exist in a large metropolitan city? Keep your mind open; there is a lot of opportunity in this disruptive process. In ten years, virtual work and flying cars might make the concept of concentrating populations in big cities irrelevant. How will that change the world?

Continuous Technology Disruption

The early technology disruptors of the new millennia—Bill Gates, Steve Jobs, and other icons of visionary leadership—created accelerator platforms. These same platforms enabled the next few generations of visionaries to innovate at hyper speed in almost every category of human knowledge.

Today it's impossible to keep up with the evolution of understanding and the speed of execution provided by new technology products and continuous upgrades to existing technology infrastructure. My gut tells me you don't have to be a software engineer to envision clever applications of existing and evolving technology tools.

You would be amazed at the long list of developmental stories going back as far as the industrial revolution, where the intended use of a breakthrough technology wasn't how the technology became successful. Think through the uses of technology instead of being mesmerized by the blur of technology zipping past.

Another opportunity involving technological advances exists where an older process or method hasn't been challenged by volume, velocity, or complexity and is therefore ready for an upgrade. Stagnant processes abound everywhere we look. An easy way to begin is to identify linear streams of work and examine them closely for defects and inefficiencies. Over the last few years, supply chain processes associated with trucking and maritime shipping have improved in leaps and bounds for just this reason.

Tightening up inventory control and flow from point to point is easier with technology assigned to surveil the operation and flag costly delays and hang-ups. The same thing has happened in the management of oil transportation through pressured pipelines. Can you find a process in your industry or company that is archaic? A methodology that is reliant on traditional frames of reference?

Examples might include payroll, project management, design processes, recruiting and onboarding, and new business development. I'm not asking you to optimize the existing approach. I'm suggesting you disrupt and reinvent to create a new path to execution.

My last observation is related to what I think is coming socially. A rejection of technology and a desire to return to a simpler life. Maybe not a 1950s life, but a life that isn't dependent on the dopamine fix generated by near-constant social media stimulation. I've noticed a new attraction to old-school vinyl records and record players. Older music styles, too, calmer, smoother.

When the growing remote work population begins to move out of the urban environment in earnest, I believe you will see a surge of lifestyle innovations that deliver peace of mind. Maybe the social media feeds will be managed by a virtual assistant that organizes and prioritizes the inflows to your specific needs.

Disruption in Design

There are now myriad ways to get your ideas produced and

funded. You can take any of the previously noted areas of disruption and crowdfund an idea inspired by your mastery approach to lead through disruption and seize the moment, the market, and the potential for wildly successful outcomes.

Three-dimensional printing is advancing rapidly, expanding the number of materials that can be used to produce shapes, parts, mechanisms, and complex products. This disruptive technology has run in parallel with explosive advances in polymers and composite building materials.

Together, they are going to challenge Amazon, and I'll explain how. Imagine that the great number of the things Amazon offers could be ordered, customized in every possible manner, and then printed for you in your home, in real time! This isn't science fiction. Supply chain management is about to be turned on its head across every industry, worldwide. Forget just-in-time inventory and delivery; say hello to instant gratification!

The current methods of designing products, services, debating concepts, and challenges norms in physics and engineering have been rendered archaic by the advent of crowdsourcing design inspiration. You can post a question, an idea, or a statement of work on multiple websites and invite the world to assist in your design project.

In some cases, you pay for the winning outcome and in others you enter a profit-sharing arrangement related to the outcome. This represents quiet revolution five to seven years in the making. It's legitimate and effective. The gig economy is in hyperdrive globally to make your idea a winner.

This platform for disruptive imagining allows us to tap into the unsung heroes, whose voices are muted by the tenured minds at large corporations and the fresh brain waves of high school students, college students, and newly minted undergrads.

The quickly evolving chemical industry is racing to create the next new material: something lighter, stronger, more resistant to cold or heat. Something easy to manufacture, something affordable. Imagine a car made from a clothlike material that can flex with stresses applied to the exterior. A material that's so light it doubles the gas mileage but can compress upon violent impact to form a rigid cocoon around the vehicle's passengers.

These innovations are coming, and they will change the way we live, much like the other disruptive energies noted in this chapter. That's why I emphasized humility and open-minded learning as two key factors to being a successful visionary leader.

If the examples I've offered up here are unfamiliar to you, then my question is why? Is it because they represent areas of interest outside your day-to-day life and work? So what? Read through them again. Do you believe any of these examples won't impact you, your family, or your industry in the years ahead? Don't watch it happen; be a part of making it happen!

Geopolitical Disruption

Wars and rumors of wars, invasions, incursions, government collapse, implosion of political systems, and the rise and fall of economies. It's cliché to note that we live in a global community these days, but it bears noting that we have never been more susceptible to the fortunes of our world neighbors than we are right now.

Since the 1980s, we've been tethering our economy to a growing global enterprise platform. One unintended consequence of this enlightened economic policy was the steady elimination of American industries, one-by-one. Textiles, steel, cars...they were all diminished and, in some cases, wiped out by the urge, and then the rush, to globalize commerce. It worked. We are dependent on other political systems and leaders more than ever before, and there's the rub.

In the history of civilized nations, there are many examples of multination empires and diplomatically aligned power centers agreeing to exchange goods, skills, and intellectual property.

Many were successful for hundreds of years until, suddenly, they were not.

When the COVID-19 pandemic began, the United States realized we were unable to produce certain things and medicines without the flow of raw materials and finished goods from partner nations. We were no longer self-reliant and, as a result, we were vulnerable.

A war in the Middle East would impede or shut off oil to Europe and the United States. A trade war with China would stop the flow of raw materials we've come to rely on. This form of disruption is never good, but always predictable. You need to think through how these events overseas pose a threat and maybe an opportunity for you and your organization and then prepare.

I spent a lot of time in uniform, from the days of the Cold War to Desert Storm, and through a short list of lesser invasions and engagements. After leaving the service, I watched us go to war in Afghanistan, Iraq, and fight terror in Africa and the Philippines. Conflict has been a constant for the last ten thousand years, and it isn't going away. I'm always optimistic we'll get smarter, find a way to live in peace with each other, allowing us all to flourish and be happy; but I must be realistic.

If conflict is predictable, you as a visionary leader should be thinking what might happen, where it might happen, and how you can prepare for it to happen. Conflict is always disruptive, but often the rewards of seizing such opportunities are bittersweet. I suggest you be on your toes when it comes to geopolitical disruption. As us SEALs say, "Keep your head on a swivel," and always anticipate what global conflict means for you and your organization.

Be Visionary!

Crisis creates opportunity, but it also reveals character. By buying and reading this book, you've demonstrated you have the drive to learn, to grow professionally, and to become a better leader. I love vision quests. The time I spend dreaming, thinking, and pondering the future is never wasted.

Now that you've been exposed to my methods and ideas, maybe you will begin to see just how shortsighted most leaders are today. Don't be one of those optimizers, struggling to make just one more micro adjustment, one more incremental half goal.

Stand up straight, puff out your chest, and peer toward the far horizon. Ignore the pressure to focus on your toes; ignore the nagging voice in your head telling you there are a few things left on your highly itemized to do list. Take the time to live in that visionary moment. Exercise the courage to soak up the mystery represented by so many unanswered questions; then start answering them.

Being a visionary leader has its ups and downs, but it is a definitive way to separate your brand of leadership from the rest of the herd. I hope you are in an organization that values diversity of thought, because thinking forward is a diverse point of view. Doing it well is a specialty. If, however you are not in an environment conducive to visionary thinking, then I suggest you leave. That's right. Move on.

Before you leave, evaluate other companies or organizations in your industry or others. Find one that values revolutionary insights, strategic thinking, and audacious change leadership, and then join them. I think you'll be happy you made the switch. I've stayed too long a few times; but I was always rewarded with a brighter, more open environment each time I made the leap.

It's difficult to put everything in a book, especially everything about strategy. When I sat down to write *Be Visionary,* I was directly involved in a battle for the future. My adversaries were, you guessed it, optimizers. They had little faith or interest in the future; it was all about short-term measurement and short-term gratification. I felt contained, my imagination set on pause. It was miserable, but now that's behind me. As I always do during periods of adversity, I learned things about myself. New weaknesses, new strengths. It's my standard mode of being. Lean in, fail, learn, win, absorb the lessons, then pick a new target.

My approach to the future has been vindicated, and I am once again happily contemplating what the future holds. If you are a leader today or aspire to be a leader, I thank you for making the investment of your hard-earned money and your precious time to hear my vision for you. I wish you all the best, and may you experience the joy and satisfaction of being a successful visionary leader!

About the Author

Marty Strong a consultant, key note speaker, and the author of *Be Nimble, How the Creative Navy SEAL Mindset Wins on the Battlefield and in Business,* the first in a series of business leadership books revealing his unique perspective and insight. *Be Visionary, Strategic Leadership in the Age of Optimization,* is his second leadership work and reflects his personal and professional journey, crafting and applying strategic thinking as a Navy SEAL officer and as a corporate CEO.

After his twenty-year military service, Marty became a successful high-net-worth investment advisor with the United Bank of Switzerland. Marty moved on after seven years in the investment industry to become a successful senior vice president for a billion-dollar-a-year defense contracting company. Since 2009, Marty has led several employee owned and Private Equity backed, businesses as CEO, Chief Strategy Officer, and board member.

Note to Readers

Thank you for investing your precious time and hard-earned money on *Be Visionary*. If you have a few moments, please feel free to add your review of my book to your favorite online platform. Feedback is always welcome. Also, please visit my SAGA Consulting website, http://www.thesagamindset.com, or my author website, http://www.martystrongbenimble.com, for news on guest apprearences, upcoming books, or to read my most recent articles.

Sincerely,
Marty Strong

BUSINESS
BOOKS

Business Books

Business Books publishes practical guides and insightful non-fiction for beginners and professionals. Covering aspects from management skills, leadership and organizational change to positive work environments, career coaching and self-care for managers, our books are a valuable addition to those working in the world of business.

15 Ways to Own Your Future

Take Control of Your Destiny in Business and in Life

Michael Khouri

A 15-point blueprint for creating better collaboration, enjoyment, and success in business and in life.

Paperback: 978-1-78535-300-0 ebook: 978-1-78535-301-7

The Common Excuses of the Comfortable Compromiser

Understanding Why People Oppose Your Great Idea

Matt Crossman

Comfortable compromisers block the way of anyone trying to change anything. This is your guide to their common excuses.

Paperback: 978-1-78099-595-3 ebook: 978-1-78099-596-0

Mastering the Mommy Track

Juggling Career and Kids in Uncertain Times

Erin Flynn Jay

Mastering the Mommy Track tells the stories of everyday working mothers, the challenges they have faced, and lessons learned.

Paperback: 978-1-78099-123-8 ebook: 978-1-78099-124-5

The Most Creative, Escape the Ordinary, Excel at Public Speaking Book Ever

All The Help You Will Ever Need in Giving a Speech

Philip Theibert

The 'everything you need to give an outstanding speech' book, complete with original material written by a professional speech-writer.

Paperback: 978-1-78099-672-1 ebook: 978-1-78099-673-8

Small Change, Big Deal

Money as if People Mattered

Jennifer Kavanagh

Money is about relationships: between individuals and between communities. Small is still beautiful, as peer lending model, micro-credit, shows.

Paperback: 978-1-78099-313-3 ebook: 978-1-78099-314-0

The Failing Logic of Money

Duane Mullin

Money is wasteful and cruel, causes war, crime and dysfunctional feudalism. Humankind needs happiness, peace and abundance. So banish money and use technology and knowledge to rid the world of war, crime and poverty.

Paperback: 978-1-84694-259-4 ebook: 978-1-84694-888-6

Modern Day Selling

Unlocking Your Hidden Potential

Brian Barfield

Learn how to reconnect sales associates with customers and unlock hidden sales potential.

Paperback: 978-1-78099-457-4 ebook: 978-1-78099-458-1